COOL STUFF TO DO

ARCTURUS

This edition published in 2011 by Arcturus Publishing Limited
26/27 Bickels Yard, 151–153 Bermondsey Street,
London SE1 3HA

ISBN: 978-1-84858-084-8
CH001888EN
Supplier 05, Date 0911, Print run 968

Written by Sally Henry, Trevor Cook and Penny Worms
Designed by Linda Storey and Akihiro Nakayama
Illustrated by Adam Clay
Edited by Joe Harris

Printed in Singapore

COOL STUFF TO DO

ARCTURUS

CONTENTS

Cool tips 6

Funky fridge magnets 8

Splash! 10

Gloopy goo 12

Piñata game 14

Halloween masks 17

Come fly with me! 18

Barmy bird puppet 20

Origami-saurus 22

Tightrope trick 24

Cotton reel racer 26

Morse code flasher 28

Invisible ink 30

Glowing decorations 32

Handmade bookmarks 34

Glove puppet 36

Make a piggy bank 38

Monster head masks 40

Flying fish mobile 42

Volcano! 44

Storm in a tea saucer! 46

Desert island desk tidy 48

Paper jewellery 50

Jumping jack puppet 52

Crazy octopus decoration 54

Origami bird 56

Brilliant backpack! 58

Origami duck 60

Snake picture frame 62

Maze mosaic 64

Float your boat! 65	Jungle fun 96
Lucky bird 66	Cat and clown masks 98
Do and dye 68	Super snappers 100
Origami fish 70	Paper fortune teller 102
Texture collage 72	Animal magic 104
Touch box 74	Pop-up greetings card 106
Papier-mâché masks 76	Paper weaving 108
Mosaic mouse mats 78	Magic palace 110
Colourful necklace 80	Bottle music machine 112
Keep out! 82	Spy periscope 114
Pirate mask 84	Pirates ahoy! 116
Carnival time! 86	Flutter masks 118
Spinning windmill 88	Shadow puppet theatre 120
Amazing paper planes 90	Clay animals 122
Paper banger 92	Mini hot-air balloon 124
Mosaic portrait 94	Taste test 127

COOL TIPS

Origami

Origami is a way of creating a piece of art by folding just one sheet of paper. It has been popular in Japan for hundred of years.

What you need

- Origami paper. This is strong, square paper that is usually coloured on one side. It can be bought from art and craft shops.

Technique

Many origami designs share the same early stages. Below and right are the four most commonly used folds for starting off an origami piece.

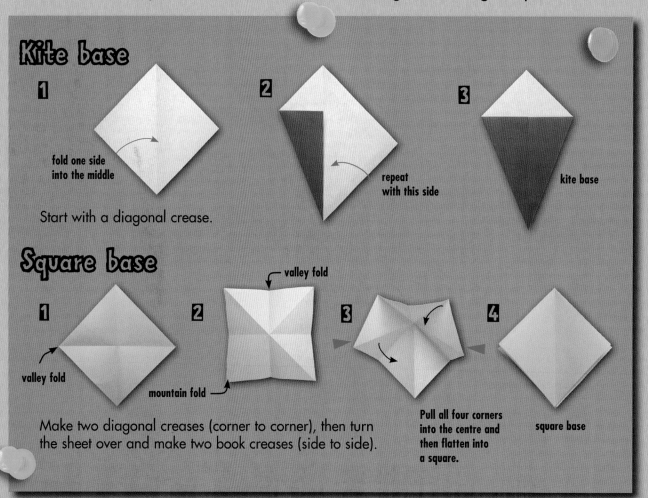

Kite base

1 fold one side into the middle

2 repeat with this side

3 kite base

Start with a diagonal crease.

Square base

1 valley fold

2 valley fold — mountain fold

3

4 square base

Make two diagonal creases (corner to corner), then turn the sheet over and make two book creases (side to side).

Pull all four corners into the centre and then flatten into a square.

Inside reverse fold

1  Start with a diagonal-folded square.

2  Make a valley fold across the corner. Open out the fold.

3  Open the square along the diagonal. Gently ease the folded tip in towards the centre. Close the main fold.

4  Finish by pressing down firmly.

Outside reverse fold

1  Start with another diagonal-folded square.

2  Make a mountain fold across the corner. Open the corner fold. Bend the fold back so it is outside the square.

3  Ease the folded tip over the corner as you close the main fold.

4  Finish by pressing down firmly.

Papier-mâché

This is the name for paper and glue layered together to make a strong, stiff material. It's easy and super cheap to make!

What you need

- Old newspapers
- White PVA glue

Technique

Tear the newspaper into strips about 50 x 25 mm (2 x 1 inches), smaller for fine detail, bigger for large, areas. Brush glue evenly but sparingly onto the paper. Lay down each strip so that it slightly overlaps its neighbour. Make sure that there are no air bubbles trapped between the layers. Five layers will be strong enough for all the projects in this book. Make sure it's completely dry before painting or cutting.

FUNKY FRIDGE MAGNETS

These fridge magnets look good enough to eat. Use them to stick a list of your favourite foods on the fridge door – try to resist nibbling on them, though!

The Plan

To make fridge magnets out of modelling clay. Think of some fun food items to make. We chose a cupcake and a hot dog!

You will need:

- Air-drying modelling clay in a range of colours
- Modelling tools
- Several flat magnets
- Universal glue
- Baking paper

1 To make a cupcake, shape the separate parts from different coloured clays. Use a modelling tool to make the ridges in the paper cup. Keep the backs flat.

What's a tomato's least favourite sport? Squash!

2 Assemble the pieces carefully and then lay on a sheet of baking paper and leave in a cool place to dry. Glue together.

3 Stick a magnet on to the back of the cupcake with a spot of glue.

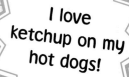

I love ketchup on my hot dogs!

1 Now try making a hot dog! We made the roll out of two colours, then split it, just like the real thing!

2 You can put a squiggle of yellow clay for mustard, or red clay for ketchup on your hot dog.

SPLASH!

A water bomb made of paper? It doesn't seem possible. So imagine your friends' surprise when they get a soaking just from catching a paper box!

You will need:

- Coloured office paper
- Scissors
- Ruler
- Tap water

The Plan

To make a water bomb, cut your paper into a 200-mm (8-inch) square. The finished bomb will be a bit smaller than a tennis ball.

I'll pay you to throw it at someone else!

1 Fold the square of paper corner to corner both ways.

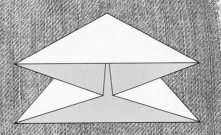

2 Push the sides in so that the paper folds on the creases, making a triangular shape.

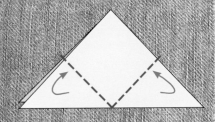

3 Fold the corners of the top layer up to the middle point.

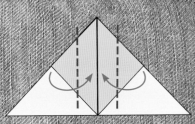

4 Fold over the corners of the flaps to meet in the middle.

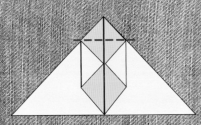

5 Fold down the top points of the triangle.

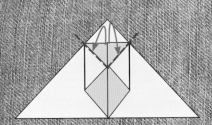

6 Fold the small triangles over and tuck them into the folds left and right.

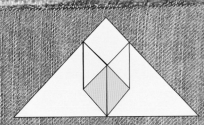

7 Turn the paper over and repeat steps 3 to 6.

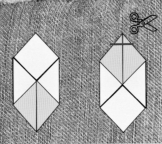

8 Turn the bomb upside down and snip or tear off the tip of the point made up of folds.

9 Blow air into the bomb to inflate it. Fill it with tap water. Now you are ready to test out your weapon!

GLOOPY GOO

This goo is gloopy one minute and solid the next! It demonstrates some weird and totally awesome science and can easily be made from items found in the kitchen cupboard.

You will need:

- 150 g (1 cup) cornflour
- 120 ml (½ cup) water
- Mixing bowl
- Mixing spoon
- Food colouring

I'm having a gloopy goo bath!

The Plan

To make some goo that shows how hard it is to tell a solid from a liquid!

Squelch!

1 In the mixing bowl, combine the cornflour, food colouring and water and stir. The mixture should be quite thick but still feel like a liquid.

2 Try stirring the mixture quickly and then very slowly. What happens?

Can't wait to get my big green hands on that goo!

3 Try squeezing the mixture between your fingers. What happens?

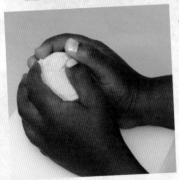

4 Take some mixture in your hands and roll it into a ball.

What's going on?

When you mix cornflour and water, the particles of flour stay solid but are spread through the liquid. This mixture is called a colloid, and it behaves in a weird way. You can stir it or let it run through your fingers, like a liquid. When you try to move through it quickly (for example, by stirring fast), it resists. When you hit it, it becomes rock hard!

5 Put the ball down on a hard surface and hit it with your hand. (Be careful not to hurt yourself!)

What else can you do?

Ketchup is a colloid. So what do you think is the best way to get it out of a glass bottle? Experiment!

13

PIÑATA GAME
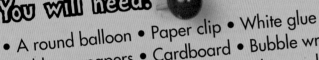

Piñata (peen-YAH-tuh) is the Spanish name for a decorated container. Popular in Mexico, a piñata is a fun way to give little gifts to everyone at a party. Fill it up with sweets and toys!

You will need:

- A round balloon • Paper clip • White glue
- Old newspapers • Cardboard • Bubble wrap
- Cardboard tubes • Sticky tape • Thin card
- Drawing pin • Coloured tissue paper
- Coloured felt or fun foam • Scissors
- Wobbly plastic eyes • String or elastic cord
- Sweets • Small toys • Paints and brushes
- Drawing pin

The Plan

To make a piñata party game, using papier-mâché. Hang it up at a party and let everyone take a turn hitting it with a stick. The winner is the one to break the piñata open. For added fun, make the players wear a blindfold! Our piñata is shaped like a donkey.

Don't feel like donkey brown? Try some trendy stripes!

1 Blow up the balloon and tape a piece of thin card round the middle to squeeze it into a longer shape. Cover the balloon with papier-mâché and set aside to dry. This is the piñata body.

Loop made from paper clip

2 When the piñata is dry, cut a hole in one side and pop the balloon with a drawing pin. Make the paper clip into a loop and push it through a hole in the top of the body.

Paper clip

3 Attach four cardboard tubes to the body as legs and cover them with more papier-mâché.

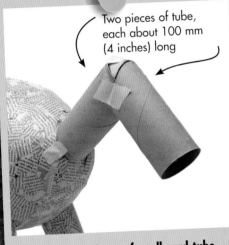

Two pieces of tube, each about 100 mm (4 inches) long

4 Tape two pieces of cardboard tube together to make the head and neck.

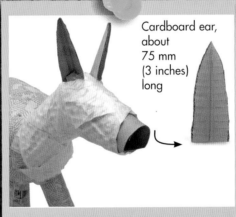

Cardboard ear, about 75 mm (3 inches) long

5 Cut out two cardboard ears and glue them on the head. Build up the head and neck with bubble wrap, then cover with more papier-mâché.

Shape the muzzle with more paper

6 When dry, use scissors to model the muzzle. Stick on some tissue paper to make the detailed shape.

7 Paint your piñata brown. When it's dry, stick tissue paper frills on the sides and legs.

To make the frills, cut two 25-mm (1-inch) strips of tissue paper and fold in half lengthwise

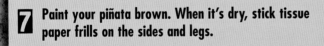

Make small cuts all the way along as shown

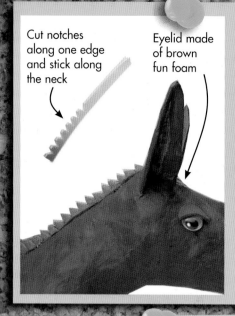

Cut notches along one edge and stick along the neck

Eyelid made of brown fun foam

8 Make a mane out of three strips of fun foam or felt stuck together. Glue the eyes on. Stick fun foam eyelids over the eyes.

9 Make a bridle from narrow strips of fun foam or felt. Glue on the noseband, headband and reins.

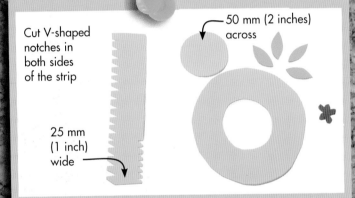

Cut V-shaped notches in both sides of the strip

25 mm (1 inch) wide

50 mm (2 inches) across

10 For the hat brim, cut a circle in fun foam or felt measuring about 115 mm (4.5 inches). Cut a smaller circle from the middle for the top of the hat. Cut a strip long enough to go round the sides.

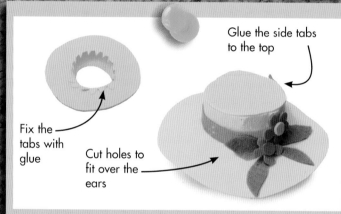

Glue the side tabs to the top

Fix the tabs with glue

Cut holes to fit over the ears

11 Fold the tabs on the side piece and stick them to the underside of the brim. Stick the other tabs to the inside of the crown. Cut out pieces of felt for the flowers and stick them on with glue.

Make sure the hole is big enough for the gifts to fall out easily

12 Fill the piñata with sweets and toys and seal the hole with a single piece of tissue paper glued around the edges.

13 Hang up your piñata. Now you and your friends can take turns hitting it with a stick!

HALLOWEEN MASKS

Go trick or treating in these easy-to-make paper plate masks.

You will need:

- Paper plates measuring 250 mm (10 inches) in diameter • White glue
- Hole punch • Black marker pen or paint and brush • Tissue paper
- Scissors • String

The Plan

If you need a mask in a hurry, don't despair! This is a super-speedy way to make a great mask for Halloween!

1 Cut out eyeholes. Make a nose flap in the plate and draw the skull design. Punch tie holes.

2 Fill in the design with black paint or marker pen.

3 Stick on purple tissue paper streamers. Tie strings through the holes.

1 Cut holes for the eyes and nose. Draw a pumpkin face on the plate. Punch tie holes on the sides.

2 Colour the plate orange. Draw on the segments.

3 Glue on green tissue paper for leaves. Tie strings through the holes.

COME FLY WITH ME!

With a little technical know-how, you can make a plane that really flies. It looks great, too!

You will need:

- Expanded polystyrene sheet (from a model shop)
- Plasticine • Pin • Thread
- Black marker pen • Scissors
- Glue stick • Pencil
- Coloured paper
- Tracing paper
- An adult with a craft knife
- Paints and paintbrush

The Plan

To make a simple, great-looking model glider that will fly through the air.

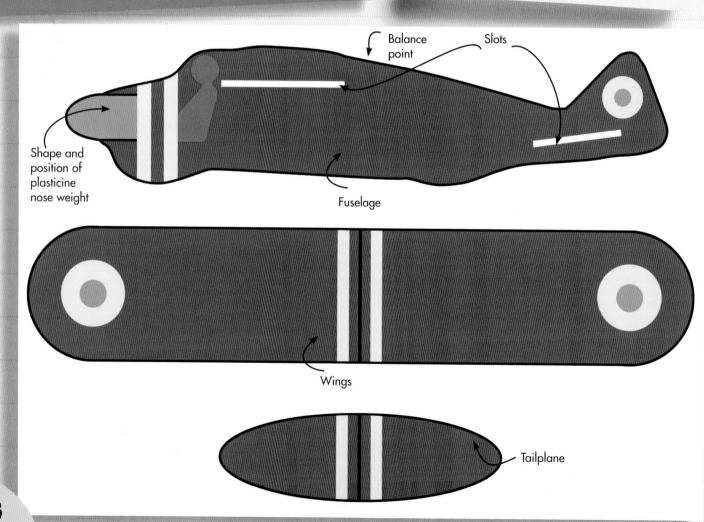

Balance point

Slots

Shape and position of plasticine nose weight

Fuselage

Wings

Tailplane

1 Use the drawings opposite as templates. Copy the three shapes onto a sheet of expanded polystyrene.

2 Carefully cut round the shapes with scissors. Ask an adult to cut out the two slots with a craft knife.

3 Paint the flat shapes first. Apply the markings after the paint is dry, using coloured paper shapes and a glue stick. Add fine details, such as body panels and canopy, with a black marker pen. Hang the plane from the balance point with a pin and some thread.

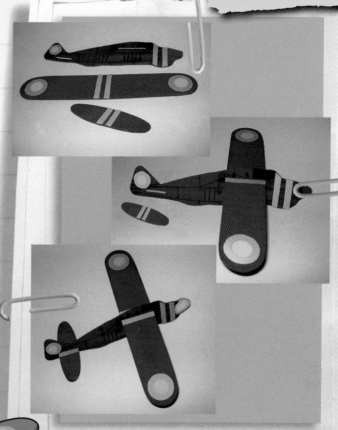

4 Check all the paint and glue is dry. Push the wings and tailplane into the slots. Add the plasticine to make a nose weight.

What's going on?

The plane needs the forward motion of the launch to thrust it through the air. The wings passing through the air convert this force to lift. The tailplane stabilizes the plane, keeping it at the right angle. If the plane loses forward movement through the air, it will stall and drop.

5 Adjust the position of the nose weight until the plane hangs correctly from the balance point. Now you are ready for take-off (remember to point the nose slightly down). Happy flying!

What else can you do?

Help your friends make planes and have a competition for the longest (timed in seconds), highest and farthest flights!

19

BARMY BIRD PUPPET

Practise your puppetry skills with this funny dancing bird.

Make lots and put on a show!

You will need:

- Two foam craft balls about 50 mm and 75 mm (2 inches and 3 inches) in diameter • Coloured feathers
- Pencil • Fun foam or felt
- Scissors

- Air-drying modelling clay
- Old skipping ropes or soft braided cord (to make legs and neck) • Googly plastic eyes
- Chopsticks

- Elastic band • Latex glue
- Four coloured strings – two 300 mm (12 inches) long, two 400 mm (16 inches) long

The Plan

Follow the steps to make a funny, colourful puppet and enjoy learning how to operate it! You may need an adult to help you adjust the strings and apply the latex glue.

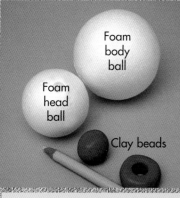

1 Roll some clay into two balls 25 mm (1 inch) across. Push the pencil through them to make them into beads.

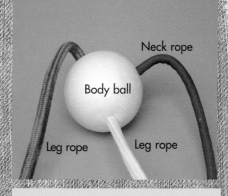

2 With the pencil, make three holes in the body ball and one in the head ball. Use latex glue to fix the ropes in the holes.

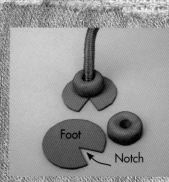

3 Cut two circles with notches from fun foam or felt. Stick the clay beads on the circles and to the ends of the leg ropes.

4 Stick the googly eyes on circles of fun foam. Cut the beak from yellow fun foam. Use latex glue to stick the pieces to the head.

5 Glue three feathers to the head, as shown. Glue more small feathers all over the body.

6 Use latex glue to stick larger tail feathers to the back end of the bird.

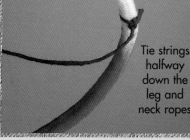

Tie strings halfway down the leg and neck ropes

7 Tie the two 400 mm (16 inch) strings to the legs and a 300 mm (12 inch) string to the neck. Glue the final piece of string to the top of the bird's back.

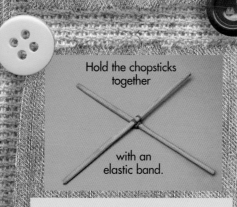

Hold the chopsticks together with an elastic band.

8 Fix the chopsticks in a cross shape. Tie the leg strings to the ends of one stick. Tie the neck and back strings to the ends of the other.

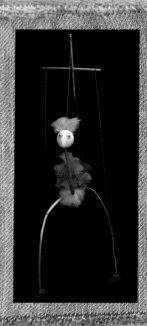

ORIGAMI-SAURUS

Are you a black belt in origami? You can test out your advanced paper-folding skills with this prehistoric project. If you enjoy making your first diplodocus, why not create a whole herd in different colours?

?!

I HOPE IT'S NOT A MAN-EATER!

Start with a kite base
(see page 6)

1
Fold a kite base with the colour on the inside.

2
Turn it over and fold the sides to the centre.

3
Bring the flaps at the back round to the front.

4
Crease along the line. Open out again and pull out the inner corners.

5

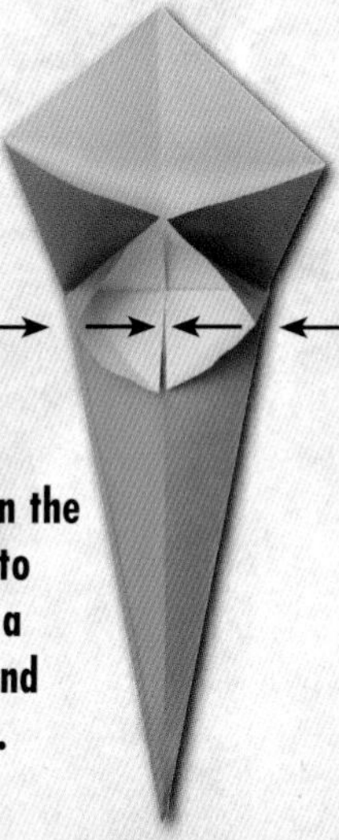

Flatten the sides to make a diamond shape.

6

Fold the sides over to meet in the centre.

7

Fold the top over to the line and back. Open the top corners. Fold down the corners beneath along the crease to make another diamond.

8

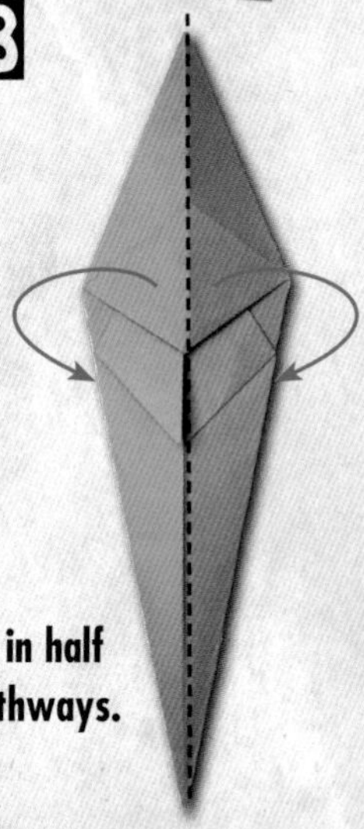

Fold in half lengthways.

9

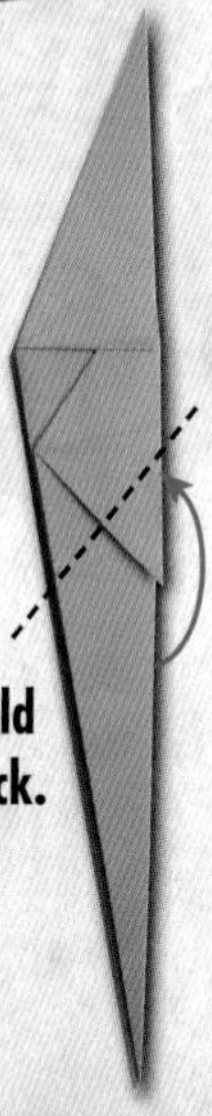

Make a fold for the neck.

10

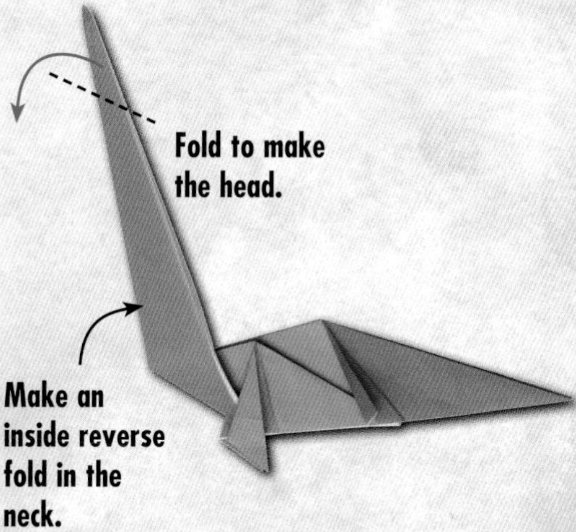

Fold to make the head.

Make an inside reverse fold in the neck.

11

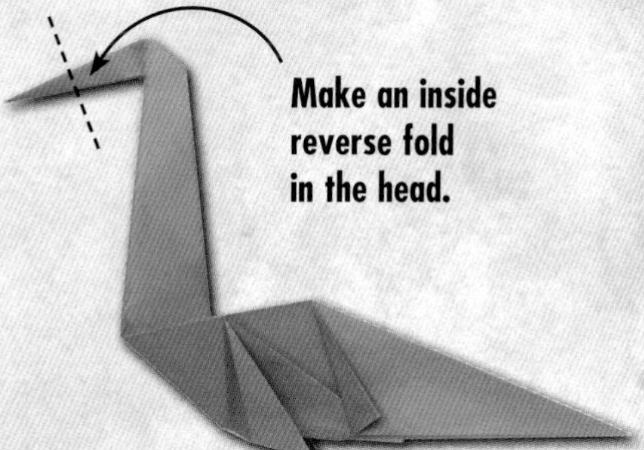

Make an inside reverse fold in the head.

12

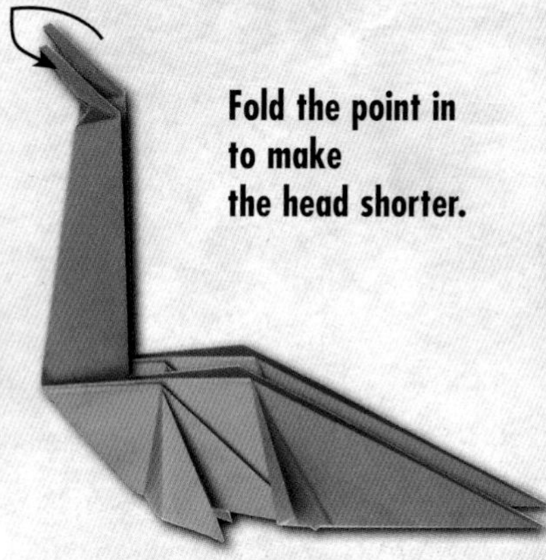

Fold the point in to make the head shorter.

13

Open out the legs. Adjust your dinosaur to stand properly.

Mission completed!

TIGHTROPE TRICK

Are you a budding Einstein? Dazzle your family with this gravity defying tightrope walker! Why doesn't she fall off?

Roll up, roll up for a spectacular display!

The Plan

To make an object with its centre of gravity in an unexpected place.

You will need:

- Cork
- Stiff wire
- Plasticine
- Card
- Universal glue
- Scissors
- Marker pen
- Fishing line
- Plastic straw

1 Ask an adult to cut a piece of wire 200 mm (8 inches) long. Bend it into a curve, add a plasticine weight to one end and fix the other end to the cork.

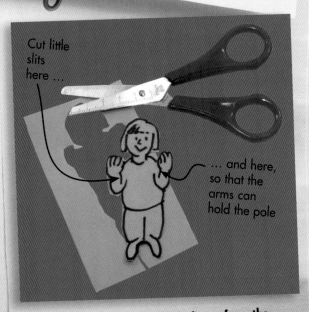

Cut little slits here ...

... and here, so that the arms can hold the pole

2 Draw and cut out a little figure from the card. See how the feet are drawn.

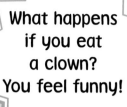

What happens if you eat a clown? You feel funny!

3 Glue a piece of straw about 20 mm (1 inch) long to the base of the cork and stick your figure on the front of it.

What's going on?

Gravity pulls the figure, so it slides down the line. The straw pole is just for effect. The figure remains upright because its centre of gravity is below the line.

4 Thread the fishing line through the straw on the cork. Tie it between two fixed points (we used cupboard door handles) to make a sloping tightrope. Finish your tightrope walker with a straw balancing pole.

25

COTTON REEL RACER

Gear yourself up for the Pencil Grand Prix! Build this cotton reel racer and find out how different forms of energy make things move. Or you can simply use it to have fun and race your mates!

You will need:

- Long pencil • Paper clip
- Rubber band
- Empty cotton reel
- Piece of candle
- Adult with a craft knife

The Plan

To make a toy that uses stored energy to move. Petrol, batteries and food are all examples of stored energy that we use.

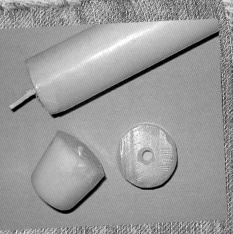

1 Get an adult to cut a slice off a candle. Make a hole in the middle.

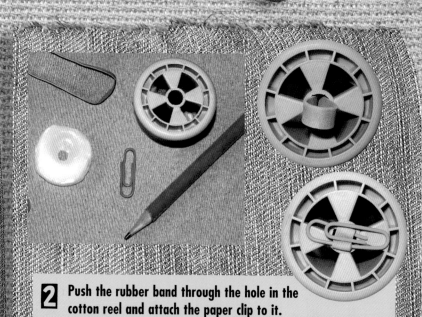

2 Push the rubber band through the hole in the cotton reel and attach the paper clip to it.

3 Thread the other end of the rubber band through the candle.

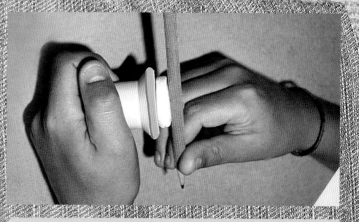

4 Put the pencil through the rubber band and wind it as tightly as you can without breaking the band.

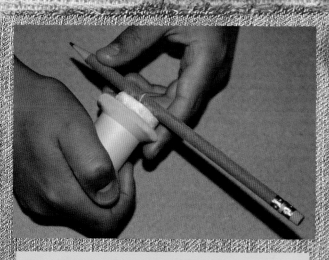

5 When the rubber band feels tight, put the whole thing on a level surface and let go.

6 How far does your cotton reel racer travel?

What else can you do?

Your racer will move over rough ground better if it has notches round its edge. Get an adult to help with a craft knife.

What's going on?

We call the energy used to twist the rubber band in step 4 'potential energy'. When the racer is released, the rubber tries to return to its normal length. As it straightens, some of the potential energy is converted to movement or 'kinetic energy'.

MORSE CODE FLASHER

Science, circuits and secret messages – this must be spy heaven! Start by finding out how to make a simple circuit.

Adult help is useful for this one.

The Plan
To send morse code messages using a simple circuit and a lamp.

You will need:

- Simple circuit board using an AA battery, 0.5 volt light bulb and insulated wires with stripped ends (ask an adult to do this)
- 2 drawing pins • Paper clip

switch

Sssh! Don't tell your spying secrets to anyone!

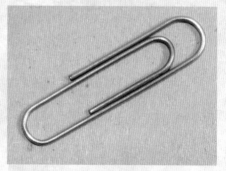

1 Your paper clip must be made of metal and not painted or coated with plastic.

2 Test the paper clip as a conductor by connecting the two wires. If the lamp lights up, you're in business.

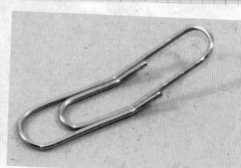

3 Bend the paper clip a little in the middle.

4 Bend the bare wire end of one of the wires round a drawing pin and press it into the board.

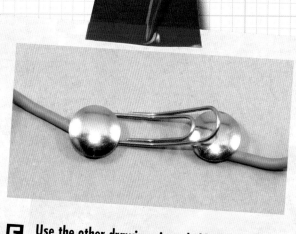

5 Use the other drawing pin to hold the other wire and the paper clip in place.

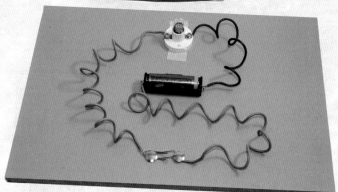

6 The paper clip is the switch in the circuit.

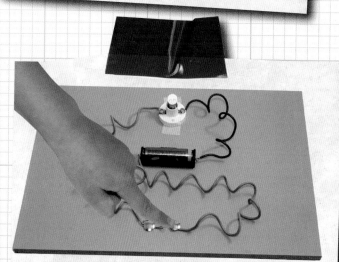

7 Press the switch to turn the lamp on. Release it to turn it off. Now you can practise your morse code messages!

What's going on?

An electric current only flows when there's no break in the circuit. Pressing the paper clip to the pin completes the circuit.

International Morse Code

Try sending a Morse Code message to your friends. A dot is a short flash and a dash is a long flash.

A •—	H ••••	O ———	V •••—
B —•••	I ••	P •——•	W•——
C —•—•	J •———	Q ——•—	X —••—
D —••	K —•—	R •—•	Y —•——
E •	L •—••	S •••	Z ——••
F ••—•	M ——	T —	
G ——•	N —•	U ••—	

1	•————
2	••———
3	•••——
4	••••—
5	•••••
6	—••••
7	——•••
8	———••
9	————•
0	—————

INVISIBLE INK

Psssst! Here's another easy way to send secret messages to your friends – write them in invisible ink! The 'secret' is in the combination of lemon juice and heat. Draw a map showing a location for spies to meet, or write a message in code for them to decipher.

The Plan

To draw a secret map in invisible ink! It can be a little tricky to write with the 'ink' – it's invisible, after all – but once you get the hang of it, it's a fun way to share secrets with your friends.

You will need:

- Toothpick
- Lemon
- Small knife
- Paper
- Small bowl
- Heat source, such as a light bulb or iron

1 Ask an adult to cut a lemon in half for you. Squeeze the lemon juice into a small bowl.

2 The lemon juice is your 'ink'! Dip the round end of a toothpick into the bowl.

3 Draw a secret map on some paper. Use lots of lemon juice for each part you draw.

4 Allow the paper to dry until you can't see the drawing any more!

5 Now move the paper back and forth under a heat source. As the ink gets warm, your secret map will be revealed.

Now where did I leave my invisible notebook?

What's going on?

The acid in the lemon juice reacts with the cellulose in the paper, turning it into sugars. The heat turns the sugars brown and reveals the secret drawing.

What else can you do?

Repeat this activity with vinegar or milk to find out which makes the best invisible ink.

GLOWING DECORATIONS

These attractive decorations will brighten up anyone's day – or night!

The Plan

To turn empty jam jars into pretty, glowing decorations! This project requires few materials, but produces really great results. You can copy our design or create your own. The finished glow jars can be used as lanterns or table decorations.

You will need:

- Two clean glass jam jars
- Black paper
- Coloured tissue paper
- White glue
- Scissors
- Tealight candles
- Matches (ask an adult to light the tealights – it's the hardest bit of all!)

1 Coat the outside of a jar with white glue and wrap yellow tissue paper around it.

2 Cut strips of spiky grass from green tissue and stick them round the base of the jar.

3 Cut red and orange circles in tissue paper and stick them round the top half of the jar.

4 Cut two trees out of black paper. Stick them on the front and the back of the jar.

MAGIC!

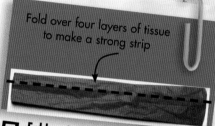

Fold over four layers of tissue to make a strong strip

5 Fold and glue some red tissue to make a narrow handle. Glue the handle to the top of the jar.

Glue well to make a safe handle

Glue a folded strip of red tissue round the top of the jar. This should cover the ends of the handle.

Tealight candle inside the jam jar

6 Place a tealight candle inside the jar. Ask an adult to light it. Be careful. The jars may get hot!

33

HANDMADE BOOKMARKS

It's easier than you might think to make your own recycled paper. You can turn it into a pretty and practical gift by mounting it on card as a bookmark.

You will need:

- Scraps of white and coloured paper
- Net curtain or muslin
- Dried flowers
- Large spoon

- Old wooden picture frame (without glass or picture)
- Staple gun • Glue stick
- Electric blender
- Hot (not boiling) water

- Large tray • Rolling pin
- Old newspapers
- Backing card
- Hole punch
- Gift ribbon

The Plan

To make your own recycled paper from scraps. Collect several sheets of used white paper and as many colour scraps as you can. Tear the paper into small pieces. You need about two handfuls. Ask an adult to help you with the blender and staple gun.

Remember to wash out the blender thoroughly after use

1 Put some torn paper into the blender. Half-fill the blender with hot tap water. Put the lid on and blend for 30 seconds.

Staple all round the sides

Turn the frame over to put the pulp mixture in

2 Stretch the old net curtain or muslin tightly over the picture frame. Staple round the edge.

3 Put the frame over a tray. Spoon the wet paper mixture onto the muslin.

4 Spread the mixture evenly with the spoon. Shake the tray from side to side to get rid of the water and even out the pulp. Put some pressed flowers on top of the pulp.

5 Put the tray on a pad of old newspaper. Use another pad of newspaper to soak up the water from the top of the pulp. Replace the newspaper until the pulp is just damp.

6 Turn the tray over onto dry newspaper. Tap the frame gently to release the pulp into the tray.

7 Cover the pulp with newspaper and roll it with a rolling pin. Repeat with more dry paper.

8 Let your recycled sheet dry in the air. It will get lighter in colour when fully dried.

9 To make a bookmark, cut your paper into strips, stick it to backing card with a glue stick and tie on a thin ribbon.

GLOVE PUPPET

Making this cute teddy puppet is easier than it looks – and it will be glove at first sight!

Ready, Teddy? Go!

You will need:

- Fleece material and felt or fun foam
- Needle and thread
- Dressmakers' pins
- Round sponge – about 100 mm (4 inches) in diameter • Two buttons
- Ribbon • Latex glue
- Scissors • Pencil • Tracing paper

The Plan

You might need a little help from an adult with needles and pins when you make this puppet. Copy the template on the opposite page to make a paper pattern.

1 Pin your traced paper pattern to two layers of material, and carefully cut along the black line. Put the two shapes together, with the right sides facing in and the backs facing out. Now sew them together following the brown dotted line.

2 Glue a round sponge (trimmed to size if necessary) to the head area of the puppet with latex glue. Allow it to dry completely.

GLOVE PUPPET TEMPLATE

nose x 1

ears x 2

paws x 2

3 Turn the puppet inside out, so that the seams are on the inside.

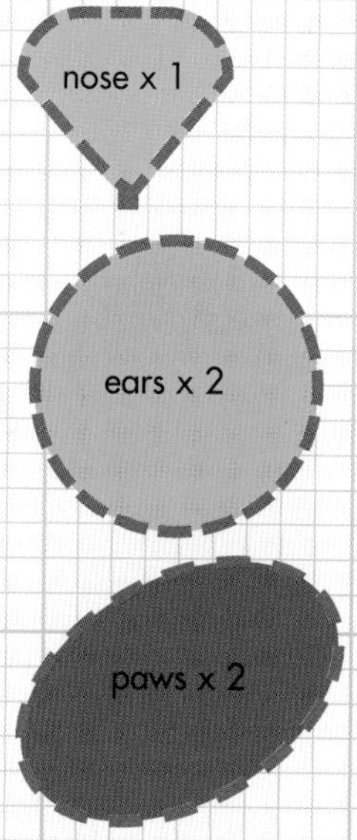

1

2

3

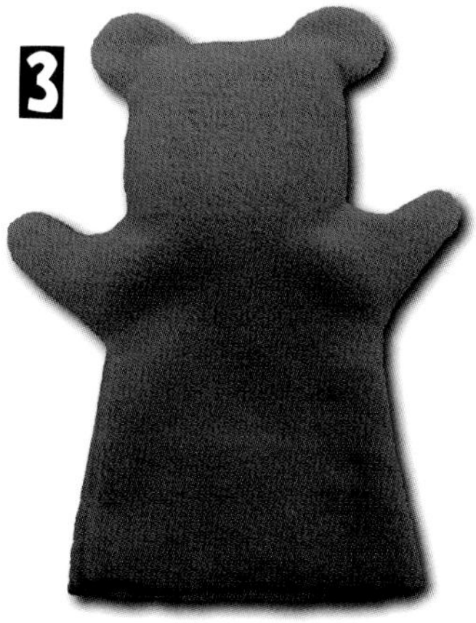

4

Leave this edge open

4 Working on the front of the puppet, the side with the sponge attached inside, sew on two buttons for eyes. Copy the nose, ear linings and paw pad shapes above in felt. Stick them all on with latex glue.

5 Finally, tie some ribbon in a big bow around its neck (see opposite).

MAKE A PIGGY BANK

This papier-mâché piggy bank is a lot tougher than an old-fashioned china one. And the bigger you make it, the more you can save.

You will need:

- One round balloon • Old newspapers
- White glue • Air-drying modelling clay
- Two corks • Paper clip
- Small plastic bottle • Wobbly plastic eyes
- Paints and paintbrush
- Scissors • Drawing pin
- Adult with a craft knife and pliers

The Plan

To build the piggy bank around a balloon. Think about how much you want to save, then make sure your balloon is big enough. Be patient. You shouldn't break your piggy bank open until it's full! For basic papier-mâché techniques, see page 7.

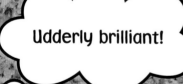

Udderly brilliant!

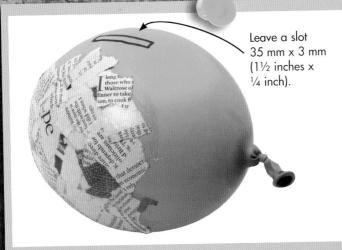

Leave a slot
35 mm x 3 mm
(1½ inches x
¼ inch).

1 Blow up the balloon to about 150 mm (6 inches) across. Cover it with five layers of papier-mâché, but leave a slot uncovered. Allow it to dry and then pop the balloon.

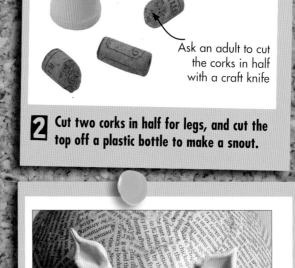

Cut the top part off a small plastic bottle with scissors

Ask an adult to cut the corks in half with a craft knife

2 Cut two corks in half for legs, and cut the top off a plastic bottle to make a snout.

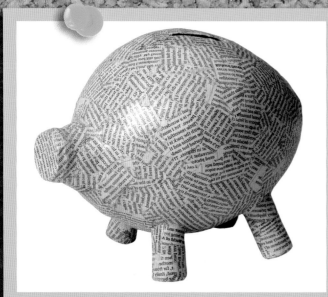

3 Glue the legs and snout in place with white glue. When it has dried, add more papier-mâché.

4 Make some ears from air-drying modelling clay and, when dry, cover them with paper and glue.

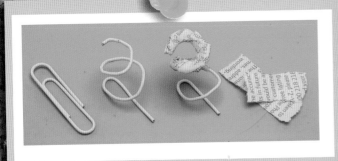

5 Ask an adult to help you twist a paper clip into a curly tail, using a pair of pliers. Wrap it with paper and glue. Attach it to the end opposite the snout with more papier-mâché.

6 Now paint your piggy bank. When it's dry, glue on wobbly eyes, and paint or glue on nostrils and a mouth. Happy saving!

MONSTER HEAD MASKS

You can make monster mischief with these full head masks.
Just add a colourful cloak to make a great fancy-dress costume.

The Plan

To make big masks that are perfect for parties, plays or parades. Start with a balloon again, but this time you need to make sure it is the right size. You want it to be a bit bigger than the head of the person who'll be wearing it! Build your favourite monster character for a carnival or trick-or-treat outing on Halloween.

You will need:

- Two large balloons
- Old newspapers
- Cardboard • White glue
- Three plastic drinks bottles
- Bubble wrap (for the bird head)
- Sewing elastic • Drawing pin
- Paints and paintbrush
- Varnish • Scissors • Stapler
- Beads • Tissue paper
- Felt-tip pens

1 Draw a line on a large balloon, as shown above. Cover with papier-mâché up to the line. Allow to dry, then pop the balloon with a pin.

40

ROAR-some!

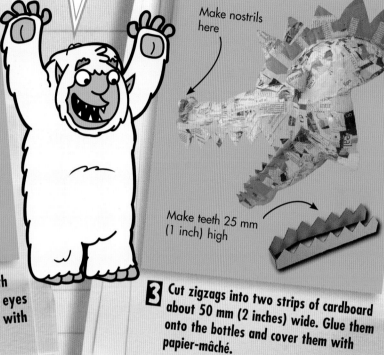

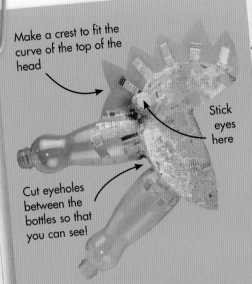

Make a crest to fit the curve of the top of the head

Stick eyes here

Cut eyeholes between the bottles so that you can see!

2 Fix two plastic bottles to the front with white glue. Add a cardboard crest and eyes made of balled-up tissue paper. Cover with papier-mâché. Cut eyeholes.

Make nostrils here

Make teeth 25 mm (1 inch) high

3 Cut zigzags into two strips of cardboard about 50 mm (2 inches) wide. Glue them onto the bottles and cover them with papier-mâché.

Glass beads make great eyes!

4 We've painted our dragon red and green, but you can choose any colours you like. Staple sewing elastic to the sides of the head and finish the mask with varnish. Scary!

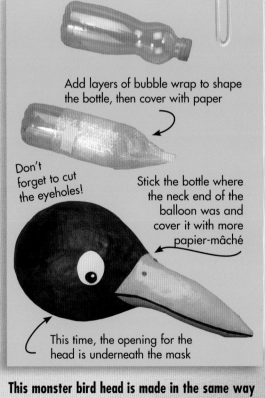

Add layers of bubble wrap to shape the bottle, then cover with paper

Don't forget to cut the eyeholes!

Stick the bottle where the neck end of the balloon was and cover it with more papier-mâché

This time, the opening for the head is underneath the mask

This monster bird head is made in the same way as the dragon, but it's a lot simpler. The beak is made using only one bottle!

FLYING FISH MOBILE

Are they birds . . . are they planes? No, they are flying fish! No water required!

I prefer to be carried.

You will need:

- Stiff cardboard
- Old newspapers
- White glue • Scissors
- Metallic paints
- Paintbrushes • Nylon line
- Paper clips

- Wooden skewers
- Coloured tissue paper
- Metal foil
- Beads

The Plan

You can use papier-mâché to create a sparkly mobile featuring all sorts of exotic sea life. Balance your mobile carefully, and the tiniest movement of air will make the fish dart around.

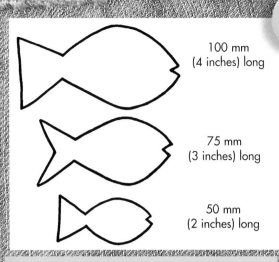

100 mm
(4 inches) long

75 mm
(3 inches) long

50 mm
(2 inches) long

1 Copy these outlines onto stiff cardboard and cut them out. Make at least one of each. More is better!

Place the clips where the fish will hang level

2 Attach a paper clip to each fish.

3 Bulk up your fish by gluing newspaper over crumpled tissue paper, then let it dry.

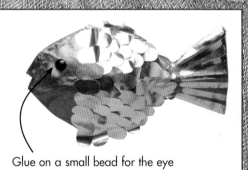

Glue on a small bead for the eye

4 Paint with shiny blues and greens. Cut scales from metal foil and fix them with white glue in vertical rows, starting at the tail.

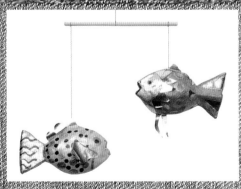

5 Tie a nylon line to the paper clip loop on each fish. Hang a fish from either end of a wooden skewer. Tie another piece of line to the middle of the stick so it balances when it's held up.

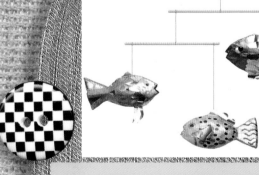

6 Make more pairs of fish. You can attach pairs to sticks and balance pairs with single fish. The more the merrier! Now find somewhere to hang your mobile.

VOLCANO!

Cook up a volcanic eruption with this simple but effective experiment. It's messy . . . it's fun . . . it's explosive! Just be sure to ask your parents first – or they might erupt, too!

You will need:

- 900 g (6 cups) flour • 600 g (2 cups) salt
- 4 tablespoons cooking oil
- 350 ml (1½ cups) water
- Tablespoon • 2 old baking trays
- Large bowl • Washing-up liquid
- Small plastic bottle • Funnel
- Red food colouring • Baking soda
- Warm water • Vinegar
- Black paint • Paintbrush • Glitter

The Plan

To build a volcano from household ingredients and make it erupt!

Warning!
Do not try mixing other household chemicals unless you are sure it is safe to do so! Ask an adult.

1 Mix together the flour, salt, cooking oil and water in a large bowl. Work all the ingredients together to make a smooth, firm salt dough.

2 Stand the bottle on the baking tray. Mould the dough round the base of the bottle.

3 Build the dough up into a cone shape. Cover the bottle right up to the top, but don't let any dough fall into it. When dry, roughly paint the cone black. Add some glitter.

4 Mix ten drops of red food colouring with warm water. Pour 400 ml (1 ¾ cups) into the bottle.

5 Put eight drops of washing-up liquid into the bottle.

6 Add three tablespoons of baking soda to create 'lava'.

7 Pour in vinegar to fill the bottle, and remove the funnel. Stand back!

Look out! She's ready to blow!

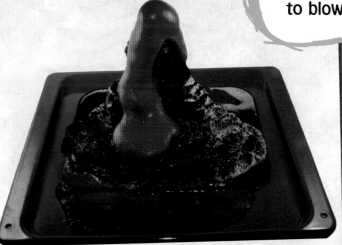

8 Watch the 'lava' as it pours down the volcano! Keep the food colouring away from your clothes!

What's going on?

Vinegar is an acid. Baking soda is a base. They react together to produce (among other things) carbon dioxide gas. As gases take up more space than solids and liquids, the mixture bubbles up and out of the bottle.

STORM IN A TEA SAUCER!

Everyone knows oil and water don't mix – or do they? Here's a colourful way to show the difference a little washing-up liquid can make.

You will need:

- 2 white plates or saucers
- Water • Full-fat milk
- Washing-up liquid
- Matchstick or skewer
- Food colouring in 3 or 4 colours
- Notebook and pencil

INGENIOUS!

The Plan

To use food colouring to see what happens when washing-up liquid is added to a saucer of water and a saucer of milk.

1 Pour some water onto a saucer or plate. Wait for a minute or two for the water to stop moving.

2 Add some drops of food colouring to the water. Space them evenly, as shown.

3 Pour some milk onto the other saucer or plate. Wait for a minute for the milk to stop moving.

4 Add some drops of food colouring to the milk. Space them evenly, as shown.

5 Add a drop of washing-up liquid to each of the saucers.

6 Look at your saucers after a few minutes, then again after ten minutes.

7 Look at your saucers again after 20 minutes. What do you see?

- What happened when you added the food colouring to the water?
- What happened when you added the food colouring to the milk?
- What happened when you added the washing-up liquid to the water and milk?
- Read on to find out why these things occurred...

What's going on?

Milk is a special mixture of fat and water called an emulsion. The fat is not dissolved in the water, but the two are mixed together. (If your milk has cream on top, that is because some of the fat has separated and floated there.)

The food colouring doesn't travel through milk as readily as it does through water because it mixes with only the watery part of the milk. When you add washing-up liquid, two things happen – the surface tension of the water is destroyed, and the fat and water start to mix together because the washing-up liquid breaks up the fat.

The movement of the food colouring shows you what's happening. It moves to the side of the saucer when the surface tension is broken, and it swirls in patterns as the fat and water mix together.

What else can you do?

You can see if hot water makes a difference, or try using a saucer of vegetable oil. What do you think will happen? Try not to spill the oil, as it can stain things.

DESERT ISLAND DESK TIDY

Are you tired of searching for lost pens? Make this tropical island holder for all your treasures and bring a touch of sunshine to your desk.

Just a thought!

How many tubes will you need in your desert island desk organizer? You can include as many as you have objects to organize.

You will need:

- Stiff cardboard
- Old newspapers
- Cardboard tubes
- Coloured tissue paper
- Varnish
- Brush (for varnish)
- Stapler
- Scissors
- Sequin
- White glue

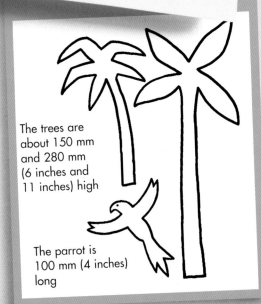

The trees are about 150 mm and 280 mm (6 inches and 11 inches) high

The parrot is 100 mm (4 inches) long

1 Copy the shape of these trees and the parrot onto cardboard and cut them out.

Three pieces of tube 40 mm, 75 mm and 110 mm (1.5 inches, 3 inches and 4 inches) high

Island base 115 mm (4.5 inches) square

2 Use scissors to cut three lengths of tube and a square of cardboard for the base.

Staple

3 Use staples to secure the trees to the back of the tubes. Then glue them onto the base.

A parrot's paradise!

Paper over balls of tissue for coconuts

4 Wrap everything with five layers of glued paper. Don't forget the parrot!

Glue the parrot to this tree by one wing

Apply varnish with a soft, clean brush

5 Glue on several layers of brightly coloured tissue paper, and when it's dry, apply varnish. Glue a sequin eye on the parrot, then glue the parrot to the tree by one wing, as in the picture. What a great gift for someone!

PAPER JEWELLERY

Look pretty as a picture with this colourful jewellery made out of old magazines.

You will need:

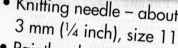
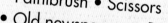

- Pictures cut from glossy magazines, brochures or leaflets
- White glue
- Nylon line or elastic cord
- Glitter • Paint

- Knitting needle – about 3 mm (¼ inch), size 11
- Paintbrush • Scissors
- Old newspapers • Beads
- Earring clips from a craft shop (optional)

Just a thought!

Find pictures in old glossy magazines with areas of colour and pattern that you like. The beads on this necklace have different colours and textures. The big beads are made of tightly rolled paper, stuck with glue. Try different combinations, working with contrasting or similar colours and patterns.

Fit for a princess!

1 Find pieces of colour and pattern in your pictures and cut them out as strips about 20–40 mm (¾–1½ inches) wide.

2 Cut out strips of newspaper the same width to make the body of the bead.

Make sure the edges are straight and not torn

3 Roll newspaper strips around the knitting needle. Add glue as you go, but be careful not to glue the paper to the needle!

You can make lots of beads at once on the same knitting needle

4 Add strips until the roll is about 12 mm (½ inch) across. Finish with the colourful patterned paper.

5 When the glue is dry, slide the rolls off the needle. Paint the ends of the rolls a matching colour.

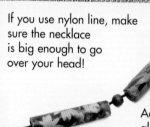

If you use nylon line, make sure the necklace is big enough to go over your head!

Add a little glitter!

6 Thread the rolls onto nylon or elastic cord. Put a small bead between each one. Finish by tying the ends together.

Make a matching pair of earrings! Tie a small bead to the end of a piece of nylon line.

Then thread on your roll bead with two round beads, one above and one below it.

Tie the loose end to an earring clip.

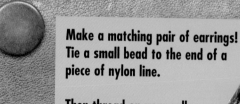

JUMPING JACK PUPPET

Pull his string to see him jump. This little puppet can't keep still!

You will need:

- Felt-tip pens or paints and a paintbrush
- Paper fasteners
- Drawing pin • Gift ribbon
- Thick card • Tracing paper
- Scissors • Hole punch
- Large bead • String

Just a thought!

These types of toy are often made in wood, but Jack jumps just as well if you make him from thick card. Ask an adult to help you with the holes and the strings.

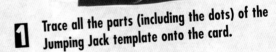

1 Trace all the parts (including the dots) of the Jumping Jack template onto the card.

2 Colour all the parts with pens or water-based paints. Allow to dry completely.

3 Carefully cut out the pieces with scissors.

4 Make holes on the red dots with a hole punch. Push a drawing pin through the green dots to make smaller holes. Protect your work surface with scrap card.

JUMPING JACK TEMPLATE

Tie a loop of gift ribbon through this hole to hang Jack up

5 Join Jack together with six paper fasteners through the large holes on his body, arms and legs (see picture below).

6 Turn the puppet over. Join the arms and legs together with string. Tie a long string to the short strings. Put a bead at the end of this string (see picture below).

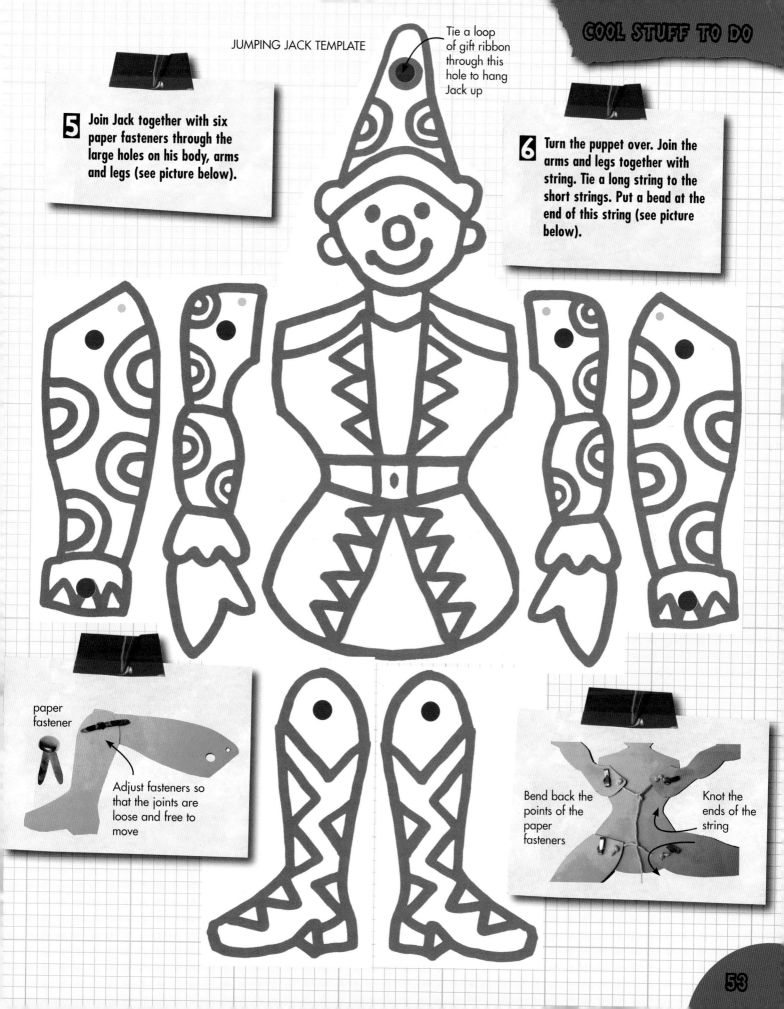

paper fastener

Adjust fasteners so that the joints are loose and free to move

Bend back the points of the paper fasteners

Knot the ends of the string

JUMPING JACK TEMPLATE

53

CRAZY OCTOPUS DECORATION

Freak out your friends with this dangly octopus. It's fiddly to make, but fun!

You will need:

- A round balloon • Four modelling balloons
- Old newspapers
- Thin card • White glue • Corks
- Coloured tissue paper • Drawing pin
- String • Elastic cord
- Paints and a paint brush • Scissors
- Adult with a craft knife (to cut the cork)
- Wobbly plastic eyes • Hole punch

Just a thought!

With eight arms and a huge head, there's a lot of work to do to make this creature, so you'll need some patience. We think you'll enjoy making it, though!

I may not look it, but I'm 'armless!

54

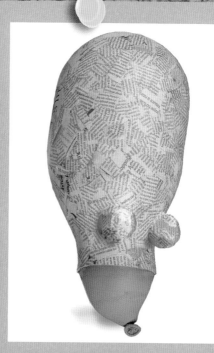

Stick tissue balls on with white glue to make eyes

1 Blow up a balloon to 200 mm (8 inches). Tape thin card round its middle to make it longer. Build eyes with tissue paper.

2 Cover the balloon and the eyes with papier-mâche (see page 7). When completely dry, pop the balloon with the pin and trim the edge.

Coloured tissue paper makes your octopus 'glow'!

3 Paint the body or cover it with coloured tissue paper. Make a small hole in the top and pass a piece of string through the hole.

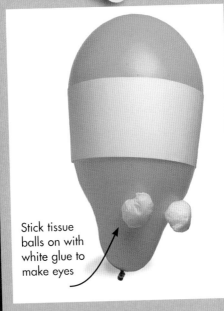

Bend your balloons before covering them!

4 Blow up four modelling balloons. Cover them in layers of papier-mâche and allow them to dry. Cut each one in half. These are the arms. Stick slices of cork at the ends. Colour as you did for the body.

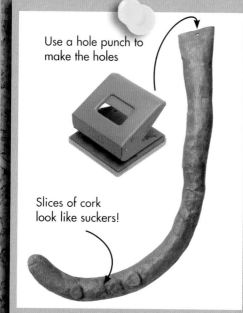

Use a hole punch to make the holes

Slices of cork look like suckers!

5 Flatten the tops of the legs, and punch holes through them. Pass the string from the head through each one.

6 Pull the legs up into the body. Glue on wobbly eyes. Knot some elastic to the string at the top of its head to hang it up.

ORIGAMI BIRD

Create an origami aviary starting with this white-headed dove of peace.

Aha! A rare *papyrus origamus* bird!

Start with a kite base
(See page 6)

1 Fold the top triangle back.

2 Fold the top corners in to the centre and crease. Open the right one out again.

3

Fold the point shown out and down to create a valley fold.

4

Ease the flap out carefully and repeat on the other side.

5

Make two folds.

6

Make a valley fold on the centre line.

7

Make creases on these lines.

45°

Turn the piece.

8

Valley fold this edge to make an inside reverse fold (see page 7).

mountain fold

valley fold

9

Push the folds together.

10

Stand it up and add an eye.

And there's your bird!

BRILLIANT BACKPACK!

Stand out from the crowd with your customized school bag. Here's how.

You will need:

- Your backpack
- A photograph
- Fun foam in several colours
- Latex glue • Pencil
- Scissors
- Tracing paper

The Plan

To make a badge to stick on your backpack. You can use your own design, or copy ours. Start with a photograph. Make a simple drawing, then cut pieces of fun foam to fit together on the backpack.

If you've got a jumbo-sized backpack, draw an elephant!

1 Find a photograph that you like and trace over it.

2 Make a simple drawing, divided into shapes.

3 Below are the shapes we made from the photograph. You can copy them or make up your own. The blue lines are the gaps between the shapes, so it's important to cut the shapes very carefully.

4 Cut the green rectangle first, then make the owl-shaped hole in it. As you cut the shapes, check that they fit together properly before sticking them with latex glue.

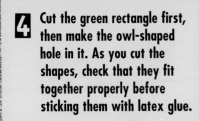

Make sure the green shape is straight when you glue it down – you can't change it later!

5 It's finished!

ORIGAMI DUCK

Are you now a master in origami? An expert in precision folding? Well, here's your new challenge. This duck is easier to make than it looks. It's just the head that is a bit tricky.

Don't get it wet or there will be trouble...

The long edge should touch this point.

Good things come to those who own one.

1 Start with a kite base. Fold the lower part up and crease along the line.

2 Make the crease only as far as here, then open it out.

3

Make a similar crease on the other side and open it out again.

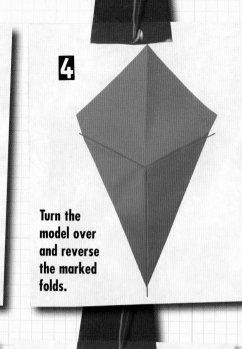

4

Turn the model over and reverse the marked folds.

5

Push the sides together, and lay the model on its side.

6

Make a crease here. Then make an outside reverse fold (see page 7).

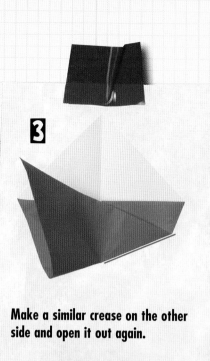

7

Make three more creases.

8

Make them into these folds.

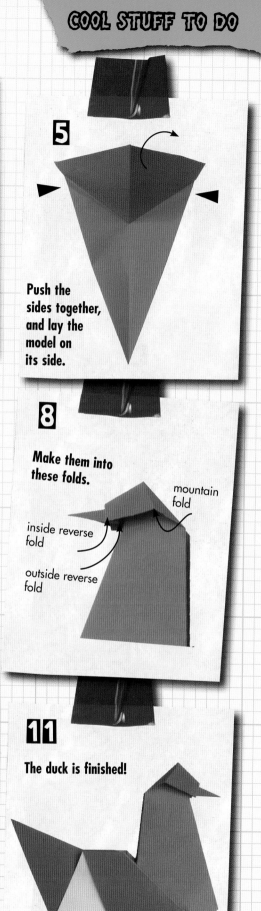

mountain fold

inside reverse fold

outside reverse fold

9

Lift up the front half of the lower section and fold along this line.

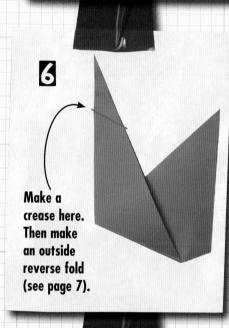

10

Stand it up.

Turn the model over and fold the same section on the other side.

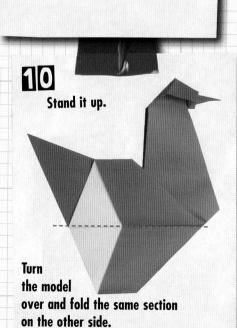

11

The duck is finished!

SNAKE PICTURE FRAME

Go pattern-tastic with these great gift ideas using a tortoise's shell and a snake's skin for inspiration.

Tortoiseshell patterns are all the rage!

You will need:

- Coloured paper or card
- White glue • Glue brush • Glue stick
- Cardboard for frame • Flat magnet
- Scissors • Ruler • Pencil
- Hole punch

The Plan

A snake biting its own tail makes a great frame for a nature picture. If you need a fridge magnet, why not try making the turtle?

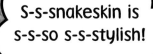

S-s-snakeskin is s-s-so s-s-stylish!

1 Cut a frame like this in cardboard and cover it with coloured paper.

opening = 130 x 170 mm (5 by 6.5 inches)

height = 250 mm (9.5 inches)

width = 190 mm (7.5 inches)

2 Copy the outline of the snake onto your card, the same size as the frame. Our card is black.

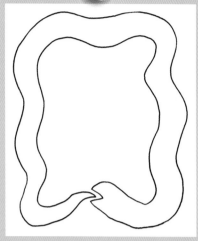

3 Glue the snake to the frame with white glue.

4 Make your mosaic tiles with a hole punch.

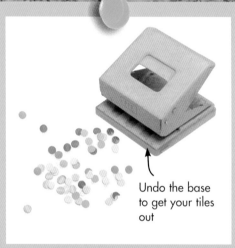

Undo the base to get your tiles out

5 Stick the tiles on the snake with a glue stick. Try different patterns, as we have done, or use the same pattern over the whole snake. It's up to you!

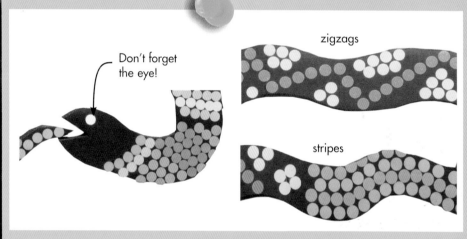

Don't forget the eye!

zigzags

stripes

Cut out an oval about 130 mm (5 inches) long from thick card. Copy the hexagon template and cut out coloured tiles. Glue them on the card with white glue, as shown. Copy the head, feet and tail shapes onto card and glue them underneath.

Use this template to make tiles about 25 mm (1 inch) across

Trim the tiles to fit around the edges

Stick a flat magnet underneath to make a turtle fridge magnet!

Use paper-punch dots for eyes

63

MAZE MOSAIC

A maze is amazing, but you can't get lost in labyrinth. It only has one path.

You will need:

- Cardboard for backing
- Coloured card for tiles
- Pencil
- Ruler
- Scissors

The Plan

To make a maze pattern in mosaic tiles of two different colours.

1 Draw a grid with 23 x 23 squares on a square of piece of cardboard.

2 You'll need approximately equal numbers of colours for either of the designs. Start gluing on tiles from the top, following the guide above closely. Concentrate hard!

3 When it's finished, you should be able to follow the path from the entrance on the left all the way to the square in the middle, crossing every white square on the way.

FLOAT YOUR BOAT!

It's no bovver making this hover, and soon you'll be the proud owner of your own lighter-than-air craft!

The Plan

To make a very simple hovercraft.

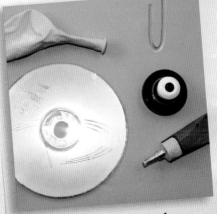

1 Unscrew the top from the bottle and make sure it's dry. Glue it to the CD or DVD, exactly in the centre. Check that the valve is closed.

You will need:

- Pop-up top from a drinks bottle • Balloon
- Small bulldog clip
- Old CD or DVD (make sure it's not wanted!)
- Universal glue
- Very flat surface, such as a kitchen worktop or glass-topped table

2 Blow up the balloon and put a bulldog clip on the neck so you don't lose any air. Then fit the neck of the balloon over the pop-up top and remove the clip.

3 Place your hovercraft on a flat surface. Open the valve on the pop-up top and watch it glide.

What's going on?

The air escaping from the balloon can't easily get out from under the disc, so it forms an area of pressurized air. The CD is lifted and floats on the cushion of air.

LUCKY BIRD

In Japan, origami cranes (a type of bird) are believed to bring people luck.

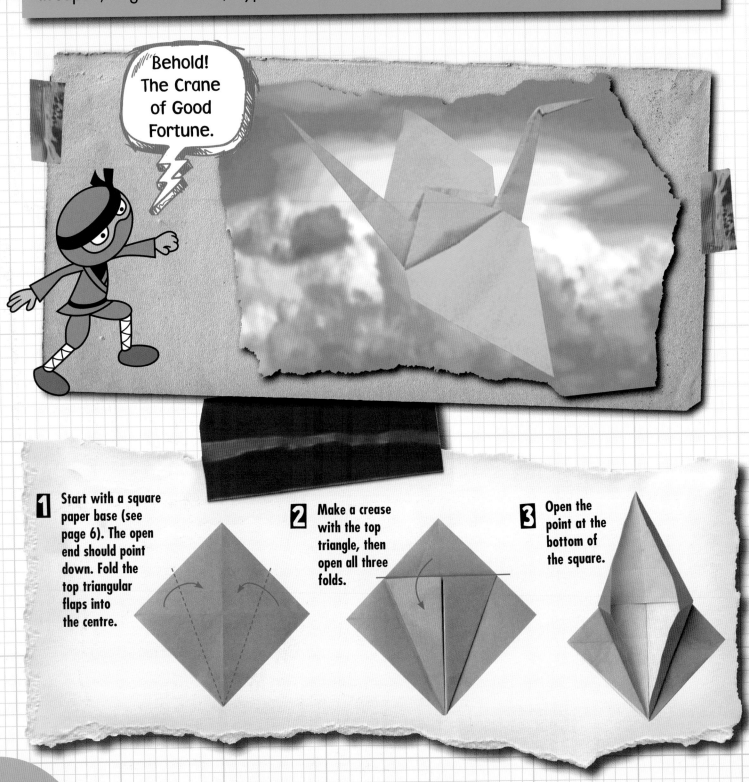

"Behold! The Crane of Good Fortune.

1 Start with a square paper base (see page 6). The open end should point down. Fold the top triangular flaps into the centre.

2 Make a crease with the top triangle, then open all three folds.

3 Open the point at the bottom of the square.

4 Flatten into a diamond shape and turn the model over.

5 Repeat the folds on this side and open up.

6 Fold the lower sides into the centre.

7 Repeat on the other side so the model looks like this.

8 Fold the right hand side over, like the page of a book. Repeat on the reverse.

9 Fold the lower parts up along this line. Then fold the right hand side over, like the page of a book. Repeat on the reverse.

10

Inside reverse fold to make the head.

Pull the neck and tail out to a 45° angle.

Fold down the wings.

To make the wings flap, hold the base of the neck and pull the tail. Gently!

You've finished the flapping crane. It's a classic origami model!

DO AND DYE

Brighten up your life with this experiment in colour creation. All you need is teabags, beetroot or berries – or try them all!

You will need:

- An old saucepan
- Adult to help with use of stove
- Water • Fork • Tongs
- Strips of white cotton material, (an old sheet or pillowcase would be ideal)

- Plant material, such as onion skins, tea bags, turmeric, beetroot, acorns, walnuts, red cabbage, spinach, madder root (rubin), blackberries

That's my kind of colour!

The Plan

We are going to make dyes from different plant materials.

1 Take one of your collected materials. We chose blackberries. Wash and mash them up with a fork.

2 Place them in a saucepan with tap water. Put the saucepan on the stove.

3 Boil until the water is coloured. Ask an adult to help.

4 Turn off the heat. Put a piece of white cloth into the saucepan.

5 When the cloth has absorbed the colour, allow the saucepan to cool. Lift out the cloth using tongs. Careful of those drips!

6 The colour of the cloth may surprise you!

What's going on?

Colour is created by pigments. Some pigments are artificially made but others occur naturally. Crushing and boiling destroys the plant cells and lets out the pigment, which fixes itself to the cotton.

What else can you do?

Try soaking or washing the cloth. Does the colour stay? Try using other plants to see what colours you get.

acorns

beetroots

onion skins

walnuts

tea bags

spinach

turmeric

madder root

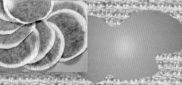

ORIGAMI FISH

Here is a delicious fusion of sushi and origami for you to try!

Flip out and make a whole shoal!

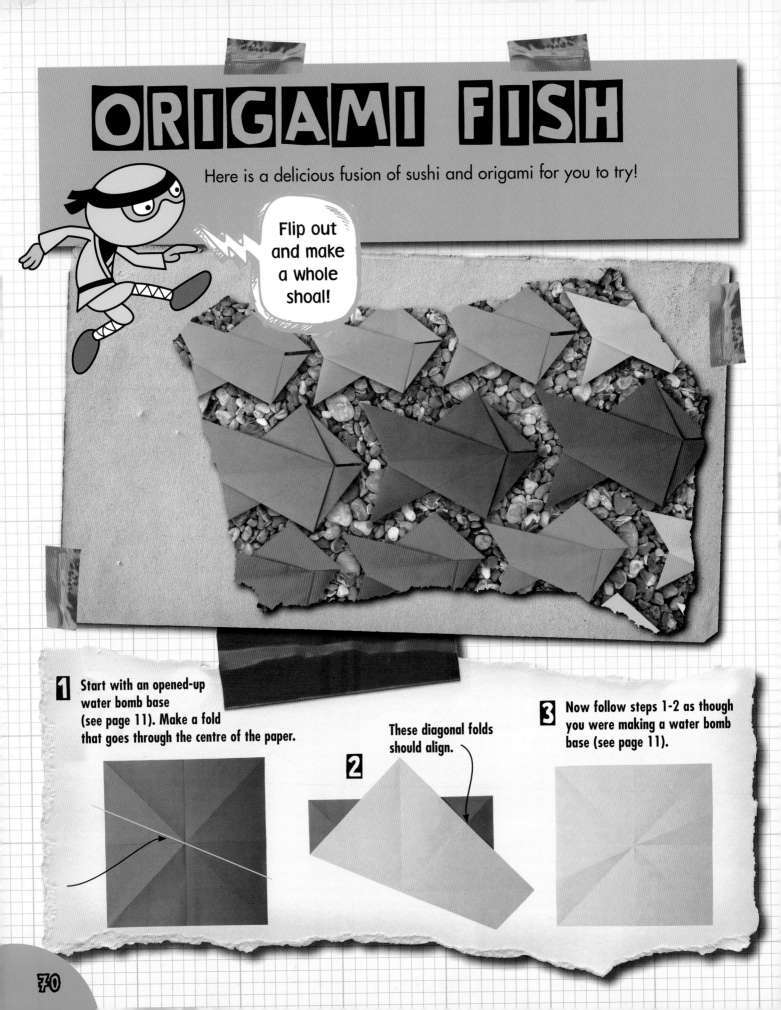

1 Start with an opened-up water bomb base (see page 11). Make a fold that goes through the centre of the paper.

2 These diagonal folds should align.

3 Now follow steps 1-2 as though you were making a water bomb base (see page 11).

4

You should have produced a folded triangle, like this

5

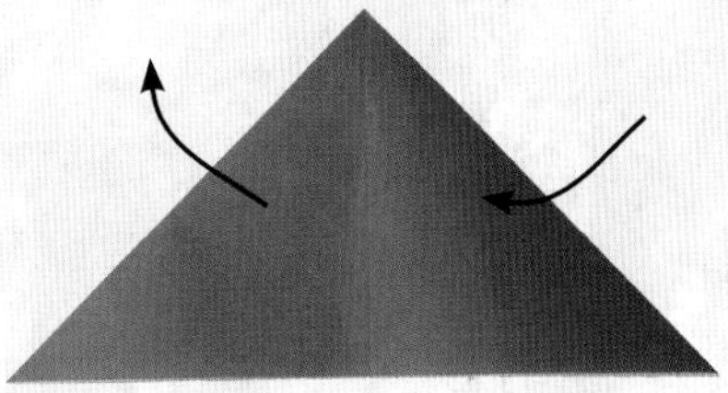

Holding the lower part down, move the upper triangle around to the left, using the new folds.

6

Turn the model.

7

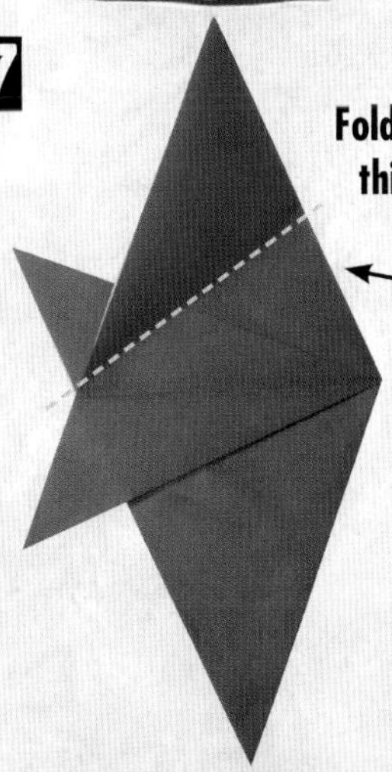

Fold along this line.

8

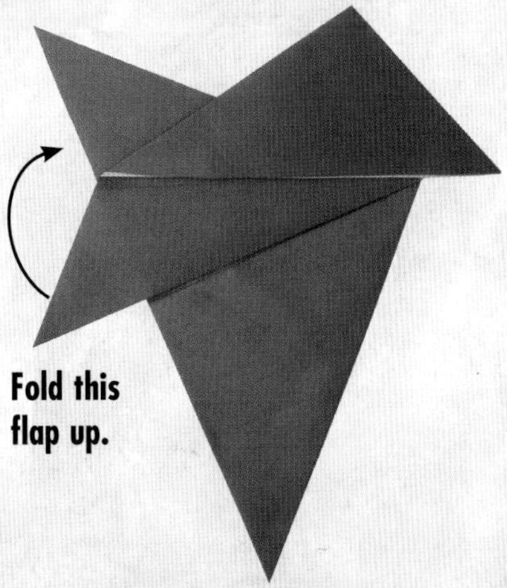

Fold this flap up.

9

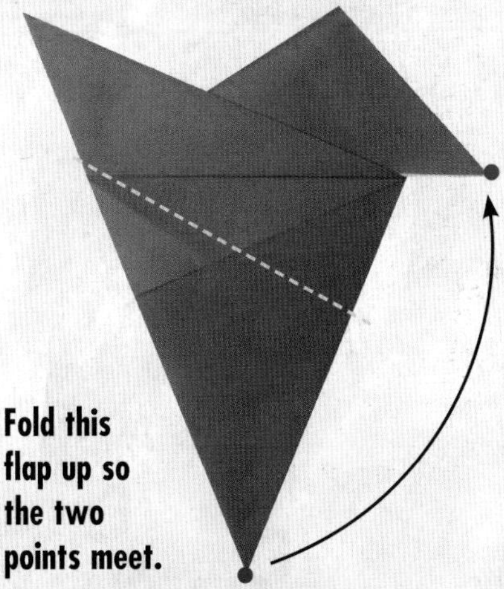

Fold this flap up so the two points meet.

10

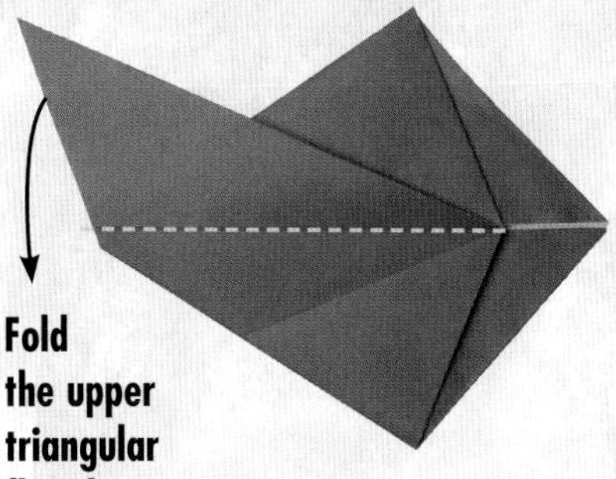

Fold the upper triangular flap down.

11

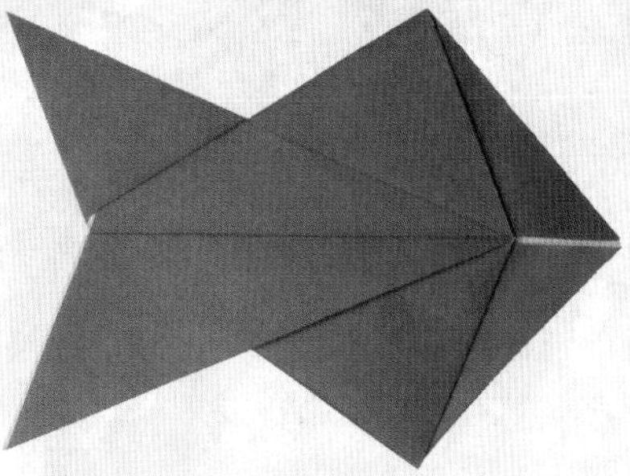

Turn over.

12

Here's your finished fish! Repeat the steps with different coloured paper to make a shoal!

TEXTURE COLLAGE

Wow! That's bright!

Collage is creative. Collage is cool! It's all about making a picture from bits of paper or fabric.

The Plan

To create a collage like this using a selection of painted or printed textures. You could even use felt or other fabrics.

You will need:
- White paper
- Thin card
- Scissors
- Glue stick
- Pencil • Marker pen
- Paints • Paintbrush
- Old magazines
- Coloured felt or fabric (optional)

1 Paint textures or cut out interesting patterns from magazines.

2 Do a simple line drawing on card as a guide.

3 Cut out the shapes and stick them to the background.

The sky's the limit!

4 Add figures or animals to complete your picture.

73

TOUCH BOX

Discover how brave your friends are! This touch-and-feel box makes a great party game. Stick your hand in, if you dare!

You will need:

- Cardboard box • Scissors
- 2 old black socks
- Duct tape
- Box decoration and colour markers
- Objects to put in the box
- Washing-up gloves

The Plan

To make a game to see if your friends can identify hidden objects by feel and touch alone.

1 Cut two holes in the sides of the cardboard box, big enough to get your fist through. Decorate the box with coloured shapes or marker pens.

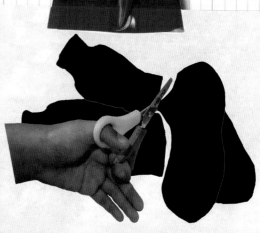

2 Cut the straight leg bits off two old black socks (ask for permission first!). Use strong tape to fix the leg bits on the inside of the box, so they make 'sleeves' coming out it. Put your hands through the socks to feel the objects in the box without seeing them.

Game 1

1. Things to try in the box: spoon, tennis ball, toys, fruit, pencil, cotton reel, pine cone, sunglasses, slipper, brush, tin foil, keys, oven glove, empty match box and so on.

2. Put several things in the box at the same time, without anyone else seeing. You can either have two people playing using one hand each, or one person using both hands.

3. If playing one at a time, write down what each player says. The winner is the person with the most correct answers.

4. If two people are playing at the same time, each person scores a point for a correct answer. The person with the highest number of points wins.

Game 2

You can play this game using a pair of washing-up gloves, either with the same objects or with different ones. Again, everyone tries to guess what is in the box. Compare the results with Game 1.

Hope you strike lucky!

What's going on?

With washing-up gloves on, you can only feel the shape and weight of an object. You can't feel the texture, so this makes guessing a lot harder.

PAPIER-MÂCHÉ MASKS

Make a whole cast of characters with these papier-mâché masks.

The Plan

To make a basic mask that you can turn into any number of different characters. You can make several of these masks at once. For instructions on how to make papier-mâché, see page 7.

For instructions on how to make papier-mâché, see page 7.

You will need:

- Old newspapers • Balloon
- Black marker pen • Stapler
- White water-based paint and paintbrush • White glue
- Sticky putty • Scissors
- String or elastic cord

Add orange wool, a red nose, and hey presto!

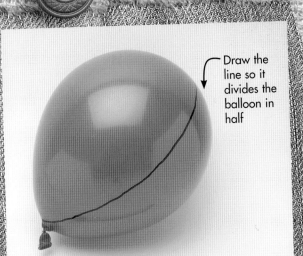

Draw the line so it divides the balloon in half

1 Begin by blowing up a balloon. Draw a line around the balloon with a black marker pen.

Use blobs of sticky putty for the eyeholes

Only put paper up to the line

2 Put two blobs of sticky putty where the eyeholes will be. Cover half the balloon with papier-mâché and leave to dry.

3 When the papier-mâché is completely dry, pop the balloon and pick the putty out of the eyeholes.

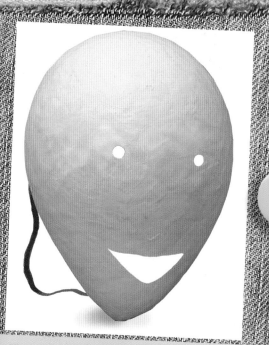

4 Neaten the edges with scissors. Apply a coat of white paint. When it's dry, attach string or elastic with staples. That's one basic mask finished!

MOSAIC MOUSE MATS

Get your computer mouse under control with these unique mosaic mouse mats.

Just a thought!

Draw an outline of an animal from your imagination, or copy our cat or snail. If you're going to cut around your creature, make sure it has its limbs, tail and head tucked in.

You will need:

- Tiles cut from coloured paper or card
- Cardboard
- Black waterproof pen
- Pencil • Scissors • Ruler
- White glue • Varnish • Brushes

A mouse-loving cat? Weird!

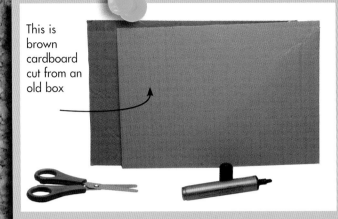

This is brown cardboard cut from an old box

1 Cut a piece of cardboard about 210 mm x 300 mm (8½ inches x 11¾ inches). Paint and cut out some tiles, too.

2 Draw an animal shape on paper or copy one of ours.

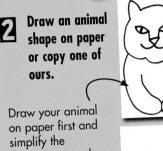

Draw your animal on paper first and simplify the drawing as much as you can

Draw with a thick black line

3 Transfer your drawing to the cardboard and cut around the outside line with scissors.

Colour the cut edges with a black pen

Work on one section at a time

4 Mark simple patterns on the body in pencil. Our cat has a striped tail. Stick the tiles on with white glue. Place the tiles so they touch the black lines without covering them.

5 Add all the tiles until the animal is complete. Varnish the mat. Do one side first and when it's dry, turn it over and varnish the other side. For extra protection against spills and warm plates, you can get your mats sealed in plastic. Ask about this at your craft shop.

If you prefer a rectangular mat, lay the background tiles on a grid, but let the tiles on the body follow the shape of the animal.

COLOURFUL NECKLACE

Bold, beautiful and brilliant to make, designing this necklace will brighten up the dullest of days.

The Plan

To make a necklace made of modelling clay. Choose bright colours to work with and follow the steps to make the kind of beads you like. We have made three different kinds. You will need about 20 beads for a full necklace. Harden the beads and leave to cool before threading.

You will need:

- Modelling clay
- Modelling tools • Small knife
- Plastic bag • Sticky tape
- 2 lolly sticks • Rolling pin
- Cord for stringing beads
- Toothpick • Paper clip
- Kitchen oven (with adult help)

Every princess needs one!

1 Roll out two thin strips of clay, 25 mm x 50 mm (1 inch x 2 inches). Put one on top of the other.

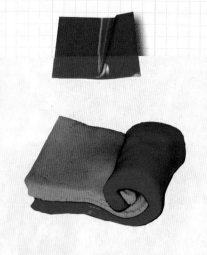

2 Roll both strips together into a tight spiral. Cut 12-mm (½-inch) slices with a small knife.

Take care not to squash!

3 Use a toothpick to make a hole before hardening in the oven.

1 Cut narrow strips of clay. Place them on a flat strip, 15 mm x 25mm (½ inch x 1 inch) and roll lightly.

2 Wrap the clay around the thin handle of a paintbrush. Join the clay, overlapping a little.

3 Ease the beads off the handle. After hardening in the oven, the beads will be firm and shiny.

1 Lay bright-coloured clay rolls on a flat piece of clay. Wrap the clay round, making a cane.

2 Slice carefully. Make a hole in each bead before hardening.

3 Make a double knot after threading each bead. Make a loop at the end to fasten over the end bead.

KEEP OUT!

Does your pesky brother go in to your room without asking? Here's the answer – a Brother Buster! It works just as well on pesky sisters, too!

You will need:

- Two thin sheets of card, minimum 250 mm x 200 mm (10 inches x 8 inches)
- Two sheets of kitchen foil – the same area as the cardboard
- Thin sponge sheet (from a craft shop)

- Two paper clips
- Two long pieces of wire, with stripped ends (see page 28)
- Glue stick
- Universal glue
- Small buzzer

Honest, Mum, it wasn't me!

The Plan

To make a simple alarm system. It's operated by an intruder stepping on a special switch, called a pressure mat.

1 Stick foil to both sheets of card.

2 Cut the sponge into strips 12 mm (½ inch) wide.

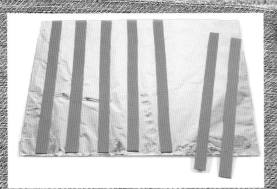

3 Stick the sponge strips on one foil-covered sheet with a glue stick.

4 Put a paper clip on the edge of the foil. Attach a long wire to the paper clip.

5 Put a paper clip with a long wire on the other sheet.

6 Use sticky tape to join the two sheets together, foil side inwards. Make sure the paper clips and bare wires can't touch accidentally. This is your new switch.

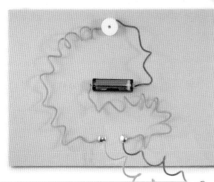

7 Remove the paper clip from the circuit and connect your new switch to the drawing pins. Replace the lamp with a buzzer.

Buuzzzzzzzzz...

8 We've put the new switch under a mat.

What's going on?

The weight of someone treading on the pad will complete the circuit and set off the alarm.

PIRATE MASK

A-hoy, me hearties! Being a pirate is easy with this crazy mask. Thinking like a pirate is another matter. Have you got what it takes?

Use a coat hanger for a hook!

You will need:

- Plain mask from pages 76–77
- Old newspapers • Cardboard
- White glue • Coloured felt or fun foam
- Paints and brushes • Scissors
- Knitting needle • Tissue paper
- Metal hoop (from a keyring, for example)
- Stapler • Black marker pen • String

The Plan

To use papier-mâché techniques to turn a plain mask into a fearsome pirate's face, with a lumpy nose, snarling mouth and black beard. Don't forget the must-have accessories – a hat, a patch and a hooped earring.

You'll need a parrot, too!

Ask an adult to help you cut out a breathing hole

1 Brush glue on a 300-mm (12-inch) square of tissue paper and crumple it up into a ball. Stick it on your mask and cover it with newspaper and glue. This is the tip of the nose.

2 Fold a triangle of cardboard and glue it on the mask above the ball. Shape the nostrils and ears in tissue paper in the same way and cover them with papier-mâché.

3 Build up the eyebrows, lips and teeth with tissue paper. Smooth them over with paper strips and glue. Glue on ear shapes in cardboard and cover them with glue and paper.

4 When it's dry, paint the whole mask in a flesh colour.

5 Paint the eyes blue, eyebrows brown, and the lips red.

6 Make the hair and beard with thin fun foam or felt. Glue it in place with white glue.

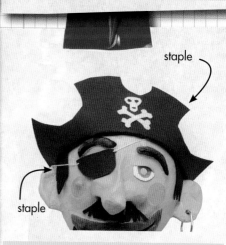

staple

staple

7 Take the metal hoop off a keyring. Make a hole in one ear with the knitting needle and hook in the hoop. Cut an eye patch from felt or fun foam and thread through some string.

8 Make a hat shape from felt or fun foam. Cut a skull and cross bones from white felt and glue it to the hat.

9 Fix the hat on with a staple at each end and some white glue along the bottom edge. Happy pirating!

85

CARNIVAL TIME!

Whether you're going to a carnival, a masquerade or robbing the rich to feed the poor, here's a mysterious mask that will keep your identity a secret. Make it as simple or elaborate as you like!

You will need:

- Cardboard • Cardboard tube • White glue
- Black tissue paper • Metallic paper
- Sticks about 300 mm (12 inches) long
- Straws • Elastic cord • Scissors
- Stapler • Plastic jewels • Glitter • Paint
- Beads • Sequins • Metallic pen
- Paper doilies
- Brushes

The Plan

To make a mask using the template below and adding your preferred decoration.

1 Cut several mask shapes out of cardboard using the template and glue onto a stick or tie an elastic cord onto each one.

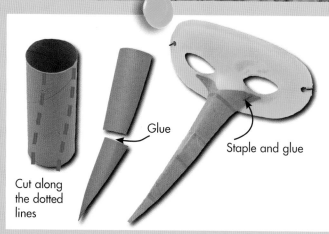

Cut along the dotted lines

Glue

Staple and glue

2 Cut two long slices off a cardboard tube. Glue them together, then staple the wide end to your mask.

3 Cover the mask with black tissue paper. Using tissue paper keeps the mask light in weight.

4 Decorate your mask with glitter. You can use a pen with metallic ink, too.

Wind a strip of metallic paper around the stick

Here's an ultra-feminine lacy mask partly made from a paper doily. Stick on the doily and paint it. Add jewels for extra glitz and glamour.

Go tribal by covering the mask with black felt. Add sequins and drinking straws for added effect.

SPINNING WINDMILL

An old seaside favourite – this paper windmill is so simple to make. Just add puff and watch it spin!

Oh, I do like to be beside the seaside...

The Plan

To make a simple spinning windmill. You can make it from plain paper or try foiled or glitter paper for a shimmering effect.

You will need:

- Thin card or coloured paper, 200 mm (8 inches) square
- Pins
- Sticks
- Scissors
- Ruler or set square
- Pencil

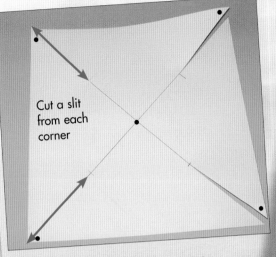

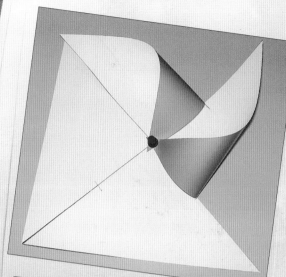

1 Draw diagonal lines from corner to corner. Use scissors to cut 100 mm (4 inches) along the lines. Make a small hole in the centre and to the side of each triangle, where shown.

Cut a slit from each corner

2 Put a pin through one corner hole and bend the paper over to the middle.

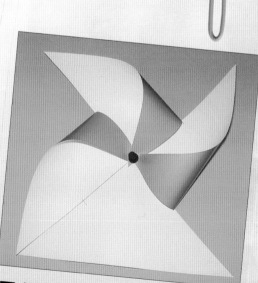

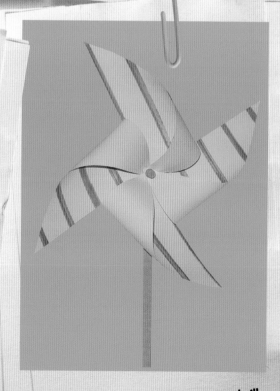

3 When you have gathered all four corners together, push the pin through the centre hole and press it into the top of a stick. Adjust the pin so the windmill turns freely.

4 It's best to decorate your windmill before you assemble it.

AMAZING PAPER PLANES

Think you know how to make a killer paper plane? Think again! The Mark 2 is more like a Eurofighter than a glider. Make both and put them to the test.

You will need:

- Coloured paper (A4 size) or white office paper
- Ruler
- Paper clip

The Plan

To make a Mark 1 glider and a Mark 2 fighter plane! You need to make sharp, accurate folds. Follow steps 1 to 4 for the Mark 1. Follow steps 1 to 7 for the Mark 2. To launch, hold the centre of the plane. The wings should form a V shape. Add a paper clip to the nose. Adjust the winglets and the angle of the wings for best results. Experiment as much as you like for a perfect flight!

Mark 1

1 Fold the paper lengthways, crease and open flat.

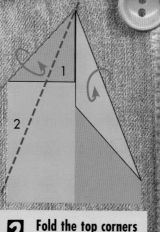

2 Fold the top corners to the middle (1), then fold again (2).

3 Fold the model in half.

4 Fold the wings back 25 mm (1 inch) from the edge.

Mark 2

1 Fold the paper lengthways, crease and open flat.

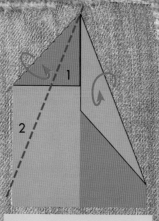

2 Fold the top corners to the middle (1), then fold again (2).

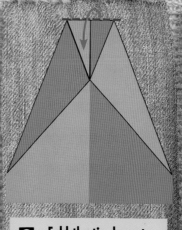

3 Fold the tip down to touch the point where the folds meet.

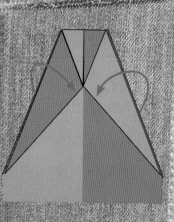

4 Fold the sides into the middle, crease, and open out again.

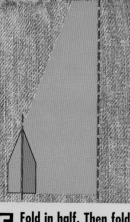

5 Fold in half. Then fold on the dotted lines to make winglets.

6 Fold the wings out 12 mm (½ inch) from the edge.

7

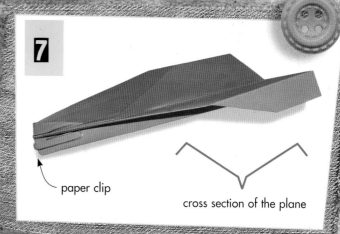

paper clip

cross section of the plane

PAPER BANGER

SNAP, BANG! Make your friends jump with this harmless but deadly banger. You'd never imagine you could have so much fun with a cereal box and a sheet of office paper. Not to be used on teachers!

As shocking as a sheep in space!

You will need:

- Sheet of card, an empty cereal box is ideal
- Office paper (A4)
- Marker pen • Ruler
- Glue stick • Scissors
- Ear plugs (optional)

The Plan

To make a banger from two triangles. Make one from card measuring 380 mm x 270 mm x 270 mm (15 inches x 10.5 inches x 10.5 inches), and one from paper measuring 270 mm x 190 mm x 190 mm (10.5 inches x 7.5 inches x 7.5 inches) with 12-mm (½-inch) flaps on the short sides.

BANG!

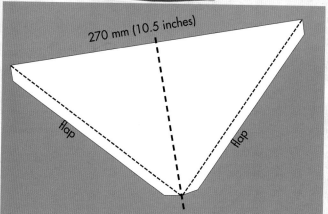

380 mm (15 inches)

1 Take your large triangle of card and fold in half.

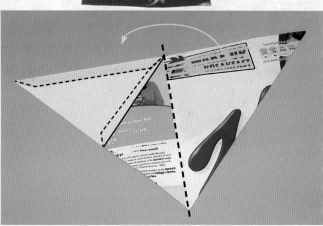

270 mm (10.5 inches)

flap

flap

2 Cut out the shape above from your piece of paper. Include the flaps and make the folds as shown.

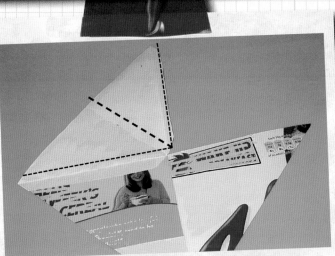

3 Glue one flap of the paper to the matching inner edge of the card.

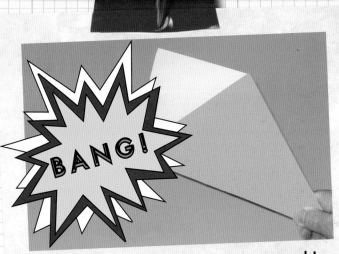

4 Fold the office paper in and glue the other flap. Close the card triangle down onto the flap.

5 To make the banger work, hold the corner without the paper and swing!

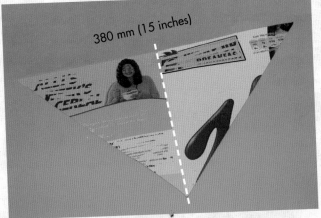

BANG!

6 A definite result! Keep away from nervous people!

A work of art!

MOSAIC PORTRAIT

Change a photograph of yourself or a friend into a super mosaic.

You will need:

- Grey cardboard
- White card • Tracing paper
- White glue • Paints and paintbrush
- Varnish • Photograph
- Scissors • Soft pencil
- Ruler • Masking tape

Just a thought!

Find a picture of someone to copy. It can be a friend, a famous person or just someone you find interesting to look at.

Light and dark tones help to build your picture.

Tape the tracing paper to the photograph while you trace

1 Choose a photograph that shows the face well.

2 Transfer your tracing to the cardboard background.

3 Paint some card with colours taken from the photograph and cut out tiles. Start with the face. You'll need several skin colours.

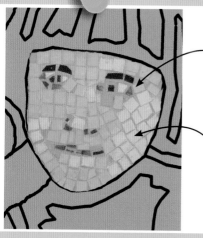

Cut small pieces of tile for details

Use the lightest-colour tiles for highlights on the skin

4 Glue on the tiles carefully with white glue. Use it thinly and work quickly.

Make sure you have made enough coloured tiles for the flat areas of background

5 Make more tiles for the rest of the picture. We have covered the background with blue tiles.

Follow the shape of the flower and arrange the tiles in a circle

6 We have used three shades of brown for the hair.

7 When it's finished, brush on clear varnish.

JUNGLE FUN

Time to let your imagination go wild! Here's an idea for a little freestyle illustration. You can copy our pictures or draw any animals you like.

The Plan

To create a jungle for your favourite wild animals. Look in some nature books or magazines if you need to check what certain animals look like. Or you could create your own animals!

You will need:

- Card or paper
- Coloured markers
- Soft pencil
- Coloured pencils or crayons
- Nature books
- Magazines

1 We have created a jungle background and drawn a few unusual animals to live there. You can make your own jungle and choose the animals you want to paint.

We started by drawing in soft pencil. Put in some plants and outlines of the bushes. We added grass areas, jungle paths, a stream and a pool.

2 We found it was a good idea to draw and colour in our animals first.

Then we drew over our pencil jungle outlines with coloured markers. This was to show up the areas where we wanted to put certain colours.

We filled in the lighter colours first, adding the dark areas of background last, this helps to link all the bits together.

Here are a few more animals you might find in the jungle...

CAT AND CLOWN MASKS

You don't need a reason to dress-up, so if you want to be a cool cat or a comedy clown, these bright masks are just the thing to get you started.

You will need:

- Cardboard
  (cut from a cereal box is fine)
- Pieces of string, about
  300 mm (12 inches) long
- Coloured paper and card
- Drinking straws

- Glue stick or white glue
- Tape
- Scissors • Pens
- Paint and paintbrushes
- Red aerosol cap • Stapler

The Plan

To make a dressing-up mask – just for fun!
We've decided to make a clown and a cat.
We're going to use shapes cut out of
coloured paper to make our masks very
quickly. Wait until all the glue has dried
before trying on your mask.

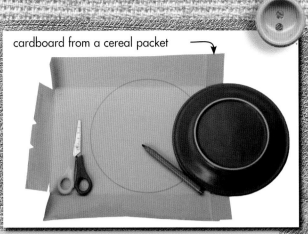

cardboard from a cereal packet

1 Draw around a plate to make a circle of cardboard about 200 mm (8 inches) across. Cut out the circle.

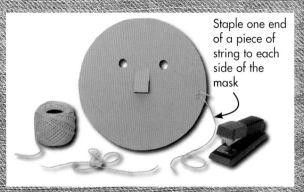

Staple one end of a piece of string to each side of the mask

2 Cut out eyeholes the same distance apart as your own eyes. Cut a flap for your nose.

3 Stick blue paper to the cardboard. Stick pink eyes around the eyeholes. Cut out cardboard ears and stick them on.

4 Cut out a mouth, tongue and some little circles from paper and stick them on. Glue on pieces of drinking straw for whiskers.

Cut the hat from blue cardboard

Glue on yellow paper

1 The clown is made in the same way as the cat. His hair is made from narrow strips of paper tied together under his hat, which is made of card.

This aerosol cap is his nose

2 Fix the hair and hat in place with a staple. Finally, glue a red aerosol cap onto the nose flap.

SUPER SNAPPERS

Snip, stick, SNAP! It's as easy as that to make these funny animal snappers. It's great rainy day fun, and once you have the basic shape, you can customize it however you like, with googly eyes, crazy eyelashes, sharp gnashers or a droopy tongue.

Guess what I am? A Tea-Rex!

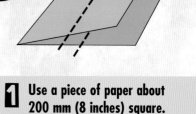

You will need:

- Coloured paper
- Scissors
- Glue stick
- Pencil

The Plan

To make these spring-loaded snappers that work by opening and closing your hand. Choose some really brightly coloured paper and follow the steps 1 to 9. Take care to make sharp folds as you create your snapper.

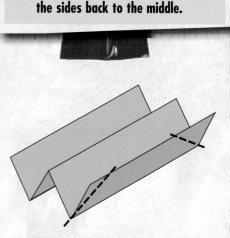

1 Use a piece of paper about 200 mm (8 inches) square. Fold it in half, open out, then fold the sides back to the middle.

2 Fold over the corners of the first section to meet the first fold.

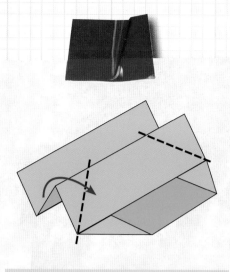

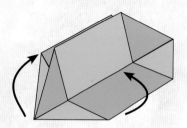

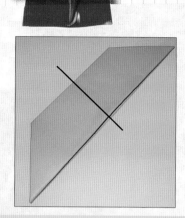

3 Fold over the corners of the second section to meet the same fold.

4 Fold over the corners of the last section to meet the fold on that side. Bring the sides up.

5 Fold the shape in half to find the centre.

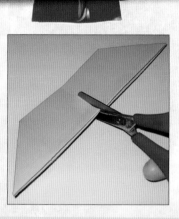

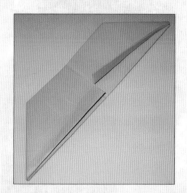

6 Make a 12-mm (½-inch) cut along the fold through both sides.

7 Fold the long triangles back on both sides.

8 Pull the sides apart.

9 Fold it over so that the points meet.

10 Open and close the snapper by moving your fingers and thumb. Stick on eyes, zigzag teeth, nostrils and tongue.

11 Give your snapper different features to make it unique.

PAPER FORTUNE TELLER

Become Mystic Meg or Gypsy Rose with this fun fortune teller. Write some really interesting fortunes for your friends and family. You can play truth-and-dare with it too!

Genie of the lamp? More like MEANIE of the lamp!

The Plan

To make a fortune teller from a square of paper about 200 mm (8 inches) square. Follow stages 1 to 5 and you will soon have a fun object to amuse your friends.

You will need:

- Coloured or office paper
- Scissors • Ruler
- Marker pen
- Stick-on shapes

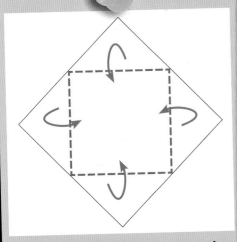

1 Fold the corners of your paper to the middle.

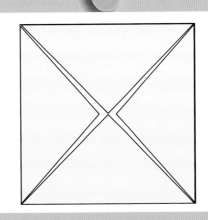

2 This makes a smaller square. Now turn the paper over.

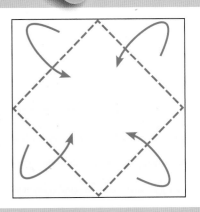

3 Fold the new corners over into the middle, as before.

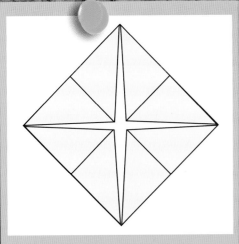

4 Keep the paper folded and turn it over. You should see four square flaps.

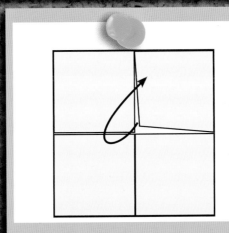

5 Lift the flaps and put your fingers and thumbs inside to bring the four points together (see main picture opposite.)

6 Put on the coloured stickers. Write the figures 1 to 8 and the eight messages inside.

7 Ask your friend to choose a colour. If it's green, open and close the fortune teller with your fingers and thumbs, counting out G-R-E-E-N.

8 Now they choose a number and you repeat. Lastly they choose a number...

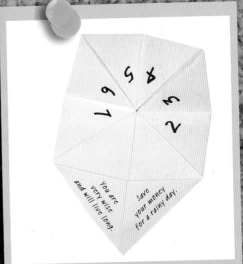

9 Open at the chosen number and read their fortune!

They are a HOOT!

ANIMAL MAGIC

More mask ideas, but with a touch of animal magic! Which one will you be?

The Plan

To make animal masks for you and your friends. They are made in the same way as the ones on pages 98 and 99. There are many games you can play with these masks. You can all act out your animal. The best actor wins! Or one person could be blindfolded and have to guess who is who. Either way, it's time to practise those animal noises!

You will need:

- Cardboard (cut from a cereal box is fine)
- Pieces of string, about 300 mm (12 inches) long
- Coloured paper
- Bristles (or pipe cleaners)
- Glue stick or white glue
- Scissors • Stapler
- Pens • Hole punch

104

1 Cut the tiger's face and ears from cardboard. Stick orange paper to the face and light brown paper to the ears. To make the black markings match left and right, cut the shapes out of folded paper. Glue everything down in this order: white, black, light brown, pink, yellow and grey.

2 Here's a zebra. Start by covering the mask with black paper. Glue on cardboard ears, then cut the stripes from white paper. Cut the muzzle shape from more cardboard, and finish by sticking on the nose and mouth, cut from black paper.

3 Start the owl by sticking on cardboard ears and covering the mask with brown paper. Cut out the coloured shapes in the picture and glue them on. Folded paper will make the markings match on both sides. Glue on small fingernail shapes to make a feather pattern, as shown.

Make the ears out of cardboard and stick them behind the mask

Use a hole punch and brown paper to make the dots

4 The rabbit mask has grey paper glued all over it. Stick on the white and pink paper shapes next. Use bristles from a broom to make whiskers. Make the eyes, nose and mouth shapes from red and black paper. The white paper teeth go on last!

POP-UP GREETINGS CARD

Receiving a handmade card is a treat. Receiving a special, surprising pop-up card is even better. This card can be adapted for many occasions. You can make an Easter chick, a Christmas robin or a birthday bulldog!

You will need:

- Cartridge paper
- Coloured marker pens
- Scissors • Pencil
- Ruler • Envelope

The Plan

To make a pop-up greetings card. Start with a sheet of paper measuring 410 mm x 230 mm (16 x 9 inches). Fold it in half, then in half again.

What about a good luck duck?

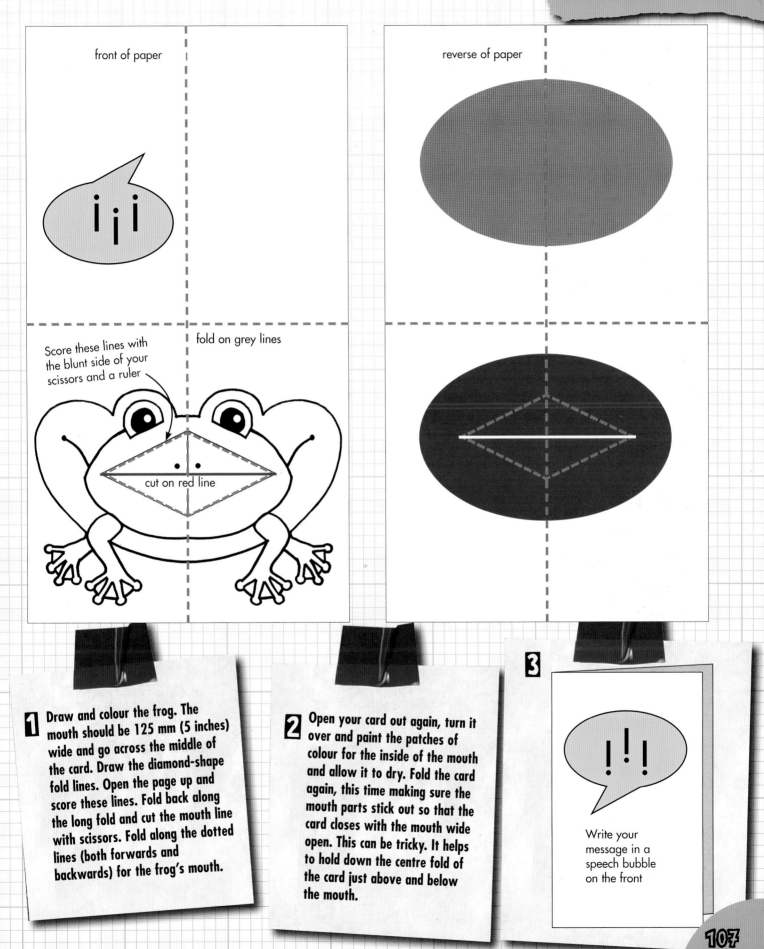

front of paper

reverse of paper

fold on grey lines

Score these lines with the blunt side of your scissors and a ruler

cut on red line

1 Draw and colour the frog. The mouth should be 125 mm (5 inches) wide and go across the middle of the card. Draw the diamond-shape fold lines. Open the page up and score these lines. Fold back along the long fold and cut the mouth line with scissors. Fold along the dotted lines (both forwards and backwards) for the frog's mouth.

2 Open your card out again, turn it over and paint the patches of colour for the inside of the mouth and allow it to dry. Fold the card again, this time making sure the mouth parts stick out so that the card closes with the mouth wide open. This can be tricky. It helps to hold down the centre fold of the card just above and below the mouth.

3 Write your message in a speech bubble on the front

PAPER WEAVING

This is an unusual way to give your handmade greetings card the WOW factor! Find a cool picture, photocopy it, then get weaving!

You will need:

- Thin card, white or coloured
- Marker pens • Pencil • Ruler
- Colour picture
- Black-and-white photocopy
- Scissors • Glue stick
- Envelope

The Plan

To weave a picture to make a unique greetings card. Choose a colour picture with a clear image or pattern. Complicated pictures won't work so well.

Happy Birthday
Dad!

To a sweet sister

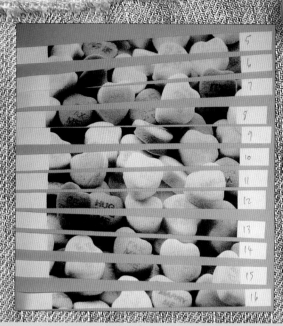

1 Trim the card to fit your envelope. Get a photocopy of your picture. Cut the copy horizontally in 12-mm (½-inch) wide strips. Number the strips.

2 Starting 12 mm (½ inch) from the top of the colour picture, make vertical cuts 12 mm (½ inch) apart. Stick the top edge down and start weaving the strips of the copy over and under the colour picture.

What a colourful card!

4 When complete, glue it onto a piece of card, trim the edges and add your greeting.

3 Continue to weave the whole picture. Use the numbers to keep the strips in the right order.

MAGIC PALACE

Imagine an exotic palace full of riches, lush plants and interesting characters. Now turn that picture in your head into an artwork for your wall!

The Plan

To make a beautiful picture full of busy patterns. Before you start, look at the details below. We have made simple line drawings of the patterns. Try drawing some yourself and paint them in colours you like. Experiment with textures and different coloured pens – we used a metallic gold pen to outline some parts of the painting. By freely experimenting, you can create your own effects. Now for the big picture...

1 Plan your painting by doing a line drawing of your palace.

2 Using another colour, draw some plants and people in the garden.

3 Paint in the background. Use flat colours to fill in the shapes you've drawn.

4 Add further interest to the picture by putting in more and more detail and texture. It's good fun and the result is magical!

BOTTLE MUSIC MACHINE

Whether you play it like a xylophone or a massive mouth organ, the sound from this music machine is amazing!

You will need:

- Several similar glass bottles
- Water
- Food colouring (optional)
- Paper and pencil
- Stick or ruler

The Plan

To make a musical instrument out of some old bottles filled with water.

1 Fill the bottles with water to different levels. Put the bottles in a line – most water to least water. We've coloured ours, but it's not necessary to do so.

2 Test the sound that each bottle makes by gently tapping it with a stick. Strike each one in the same place. Can you play a tune?

3 Using the same set of bottles, blow across the top of each bottle in turn. Try to get a clear note.

4 Now try to play *Ten Green Bottles!*

What else can you do?

You could make two sets of bottles to play duets with a friend – one set for hitting, one for blowing!

What's going on?

Why does the fullest bottle have the highest sound when you blow it, but the lowest sound when you hit it?

Well, sound is made by creating vibrations, which are carried as waves through the air to our ears.

In Step 2, the sound is made by a sharp blow of the stick making the combination of water and glass vibrate. The more water there is in the bottle, the lower the pitch, and the less water, the higher the pitch.

In Step 3, the sound is made by vibrating a volume of air. The greater the volume of air, the lower the pitch, and the smaller the volume of air, the higher – exactly the opposite result to Step 2.

That music's out of this world!

113

SPY PERISCOPE

Like all the best spy gadgets, this one looks like something very ordinary, but it can do extraordinary things! Use it to stay unseen while you snoop, or peek over the heads of crowds.

SURPRISE! I saw you first!

You will need:

- Empty carton – a clean, dry fruit juice carton or similar-sized box
- 2 plastic mirrors – each about 75 mm x 50 mm (3 inches x 2 inches) • Ruler • Scissors
- Marker pen • Parcel tape

The Plan

To make a simple periscope.

2 Measure the diagonal (X). Using the ruler, draw the outline of a square flap on the bottom of the front of the box (black line). Take care to use the same measurement (X) for the height and width of the flap.

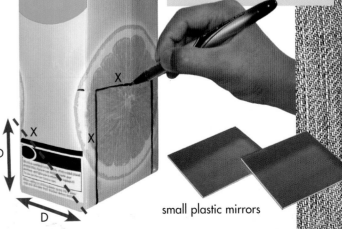

small plastic mirrors

1 Remove any plastic spout and seal the carton with tape. Measure the depth of the carton (D) and mark the same distance up the side.

3 Carefully cut three sides of the flap and fold inwards. Use sticky tape to fix the flap at a 45° slant.

4 Cut a flap at the top of the box on the other side, the same size (X by X) as before. Fix this flap, again at a 45° slant, with tape.

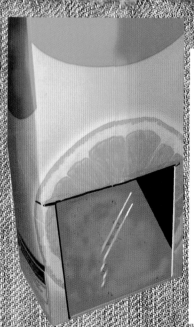

mirror 45°

Path of light

mirror 45°

5 Stick one mirror to each flap with some universal glue.

6 Now test your periscope!

PIRATES AHOY!

Make this unusual card on a pirate theme.
It's a complete adventure story in a card!

You will need:

- Coloured paper • Thin card • Scissors
- Coloured marker pens • Glue stick
- Fine black marker pen
- Large envelope

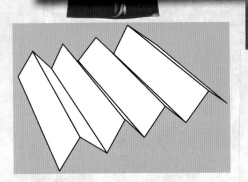

1 Fold your thin card as shown. Now trace or copy the sea template onto blue paper and cut out. Cut along the wavy line to make two sets of waves.

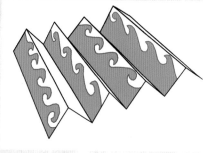

2 Repeat this for four sets. Trim the sides to fit the card. The tops of the waves should be just below the folds. Stick them on as shown.

3 Start with the pirate captain from the templates. Cut him out in card and add coloured paper for his clothes, or colour him in with markers. Draw the details with a fine black marker pen. Glue the tab shown in yellow on the template.

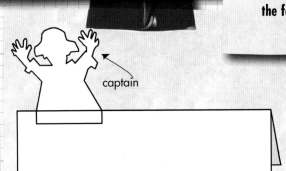

captain

4 Attach it to the back of the first zigzag. Glue the other cutouts in place. The mate doesn't have a tab. Stick him on the front of the first wave.

5 Adjust your card as shown, so that the zigzag stands up. Fold it up to go in the envelope. Don't forget to write a message!

FLUTTER MASKS

These masks are perfect for when you receive an invitation to the Butterfly's Ball. If you don't, why not hold your own?

The Plan

The red dotted line on this page is one half of a butterfly, the purple one on the right is one half of a moth. Choose your shape, trace it onto a piece of paper and cut it out. This is your template. Adjust the eyeholes if you need to, so you can see clearly.

You will need:

- Stiff cardboard, about 440 mm x 270 mm (17.5 inches by 10.5 inches)
- Coloured paper
- Tracing paper
- Paper clip • Plastic bottle
- Pencil
- Glue stick • Scissors

eyehole of butterfly

centre line of butterfly

Butterflies are beautiful, but bugs are best!

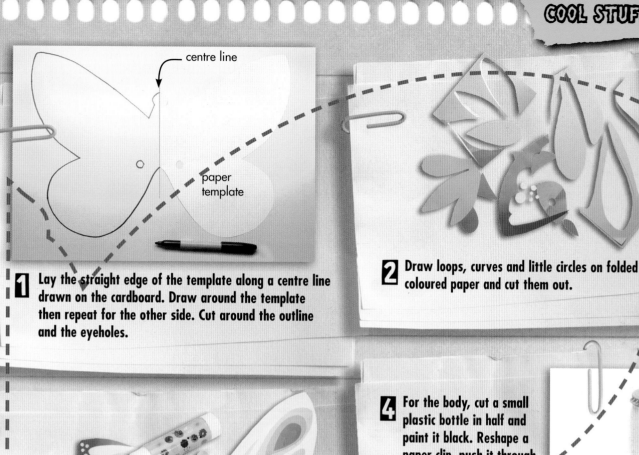

1 Lay the straight edge of the template along a centre line drawn on the cardboard. Draw around the template then repeat for the other side. Cut around the outline and the eyeholes.

centre line

paper template

2 Draw loops, curves and little circles on folded coloured paper and cut them out.

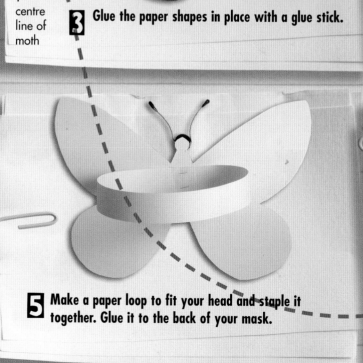

eyehole of moth →

centre line of moth

3 Glue the paper shapes in place with a glue stick.

4 For the body, cut a small plastic bottle in half and paint it black. Reshape a paper clip, push it through a black bead and add two blobs of modelling clay to make the head and antennae.

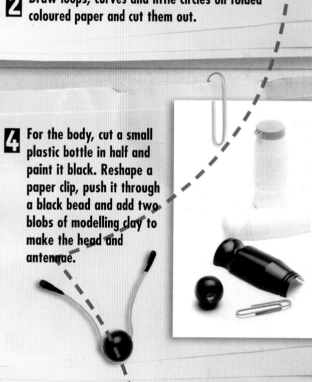

5 Make a paper loop to fit your head and staple it together. Glue it to the back of your mask.

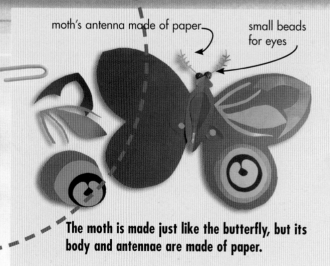

moth's antenna made of paper

small beads for eyes

The moth is made just like the butterfly, but its body and antennae are made of paper.

SHADOW PUPPET THEATRE

Shadow plays feature in at least 20 cultures worldwide. Capture the drama here!

You will need:

- Cardboard box • Tracing paper
- Hard black card • Paper fasteners
- Paint and paintbrush • Tape
- Hole punch • Pencil • Scissors
- Pen • Ruler • Adult with a craft knife
- Barbecue skewers • White glue
- Desk lamp or big torch

The Plan

To make a theatre out of a cardboard box. The box should be 300 mm x 230 mm x 230 mm (12 inches x 9 inches x 9 inches).

1 Copy and cut out the shapes above and opposite. Put seven paper fasteners through the holes, joining A to A, B to B and so on.

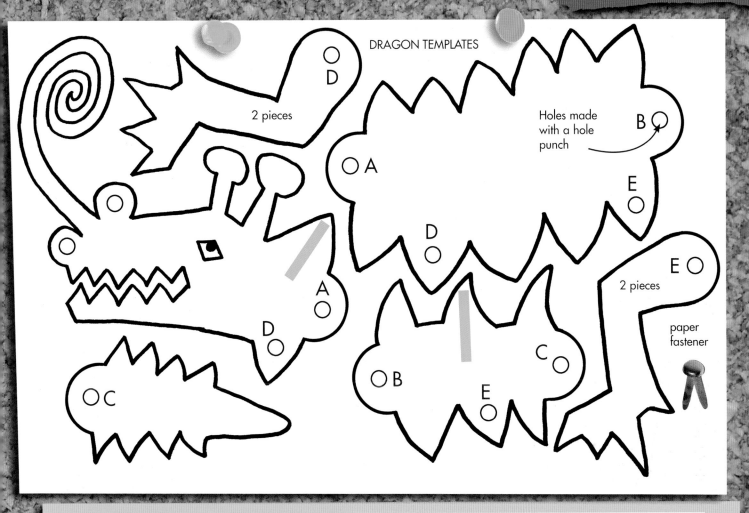

DRAGON TEMPLATES

2 pieces

D

○A

Holes made with a hole punch

B ○

E ○

D ○

2 pieces

E ○

paper fastener

A ○

D ○

○ C

B ○

E ○

C ○

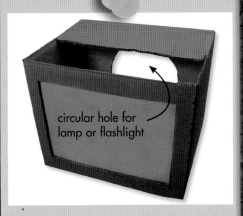

2 Glue the ends of the barbecue skewers where the green bars are shown. You can control your dragon by moving the ends of the sticks.

Draw a line about 50 mm (2 inches) from the edges

3 Cut off the front and side flaps of the box with scissors. Mark a rectangle as shown above.

circular hole for lamp or flashlight

4 Ask an adult to cut holes at the front and back with a craft knife. Paint the outside of the box. Tape tracing paper inside the front to make the screen.

5 Shine a light towards the front and move your puppets close to the screen. Let the battle begin!

CLAY ANIMALS

Let's make some clay collectables. We've chosen to make an elephant, a piglet, a snail and a little bear. You can choose to make any animals you like.

My favourite food... Baked beings!

The Plan

To make little animals from modelling clay. Copy ours or make your own. If you want to make eyes for your animals, make sure you've got some black and white clay.

You will need:

- Modelling clay
- Modelling tools
- Plastic bag and sticky tape
- Plastic wobbly eyes (optional)
- Kitchen stove (with adult help)

1 The elephant has nine pieces. Make the body, tail and four legs. Now make a head and trunk as one piece. Make two ears. Join the legs and tail to the body. Push his head on and curl his trunk up. Press on both his ears. Add his eyes, tweak his tail!

2 Piglet is made from eight pieces of clay. Make his head and body from one piece. Flatten one end to make his snout. Use clay tools to mark his mouth and nostrils. Pinch the ear flaps before you fix them on. Don't forget to put a twist in his little tail.

3 Use four colours to make the snail. Roll out brown, white and black into lengths. Twist the lengths together to make his shell. Use fawn clay for his body. Create his eyes from black and white clay. Make a cut for his mouth. Press the shell onto his body to complete the snail.

4 This bear is made from eight pieces of brown clay. Press the arms and legs onto his body. Fix his head and ears. Add a black button nose and two eyes. Shape his mouth with a modelling tool. Bake your animals in the oven until hard, then leave to cool.

MINI HOT-AIR BALLOON

Have you ever looked at a hot-air balloon in the sky and wondered how it stays up there? Well, here's how.

You will need:

- Card • Marker pen • Scissors
- Glue stick • Paper clips
- About 450 mm (18 inches) of thin wire
- Hairdryer • Sticky tape • Long pole
- Cardboard or plastic tube (the sort used for mailing posters would do)

The Plan

To make a balloon powered by hot air.

Up, up and away!

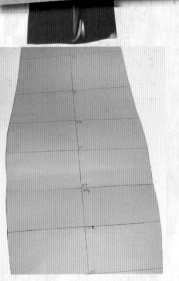

1 Copy the shape opposite onto card. You will probably have to stick several sheets together. Make your card 1,220 mm x 280 mm (48 inches x 11 inches), then draw a centre line. Centre each measurement on this line. Draw the outline, then cut it out. This is your template.

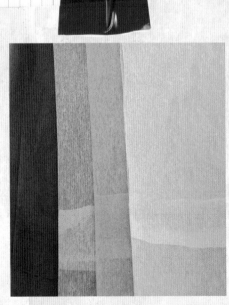

2 The panels of the balloon are eight pieces of tissue paper each measuring 1,220 mm x 280 mm (48 inches x 11 inches). You may have to stick sheets together for this.

3 Make a stack of the eight panels and fasten them together at the corners with paper clips.

4 Lay the card template on the stack. Carefully draw round the template with a marker pen.

124

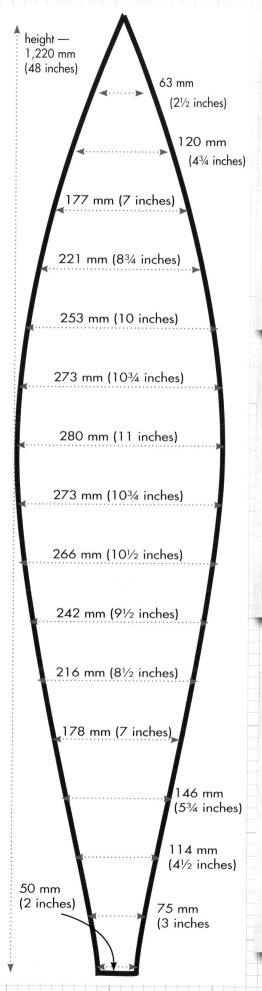

height —
1,220 mm
(48 inches)

63 mm
(2½ inches)

120 mm
(4¾ inches)

177 mm (7 inches)

221 mm (8¾ inches)

253 mm (10 inches)

273 mm (10¾ inches)

280 mm (11 inches)

273 mm (10¾ inches)

266 mm (10½ inches)

242 mm (9½ inches)

216 mm (8½ inches)

178 mm (7 inches)

146 mm
(5¾ inches)

114 mm
(4½ inches)

50 mm
(2 inches)

75 mm
(3 inches

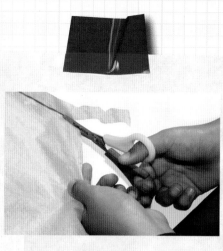

5 Use scissors to cut round your guide line.

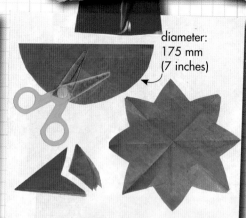

diameter:
175 mm
(7 inches)

6 Cut a circle from tissue, fold in half twice and cut out a V shape as shown.

7 Use two panels and lay one on top of the other, but about 9 mm (½ inch) to one side. Put glue on the edge of the lower panel and fold it over the top one.

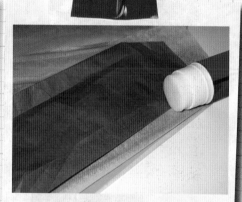

8 Put on a third piece, moving it 9 mm (½ inch) back in the opposite direction to the last one.

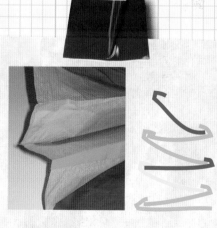

9 Continue glueing layers, until you have all eight stuck together. Seen from the end, the stack should look like the diagram above.

10 Check that everything is stuck correctly. Finish by folding the middle of the stack inwards and out of the way, then glue and fold the last seam.

11 Cut 25-mm (1-inch) deep tabs in the base of each panel.

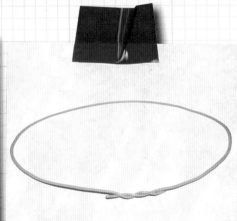

12 Make a ring from the wire. Fit it inside the neck of the balloon.

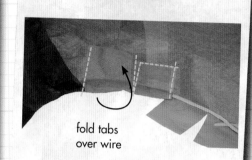

fold tabs over wire

13 Wrap the tabs round the ring and glue.

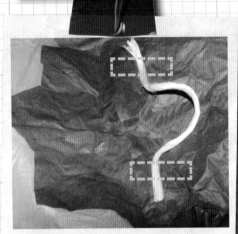

14 Glue the star shape on the top. Attach a loop of string with tape.

15 Use a pole to support the balloon.

16

Inflate the balloon with the hairdryer and tube. Mend any holes with glue and tissue. Finish filling the balloon with hot air.

17

Enjoy the flight!

What's going on?

Hot air expands and is lighter than the surrounding air. When the difference is great enough, it can lift itself and the weight of the balloon that contains it.

TASTE TEST

The Taste Test is a great party game to play with friends. We are using crisps but you can try other foods, such as tomato ketchup, jam, lemon juice and melted chocolate! See what happens when you use a blindfold and block your nose. The results could surprise you.

> Block your nose and my food will taste great!

The Plan

To play a game to see how well your friends can tell what they're eating by taste alone. Then play again allowing them to smell.

You will need:

- 4 different crisp flavours
- Blindfold
- Notebook and pencil

What's going on?

We can only taste five things: bitter, salty, sweet, sour and umami (savoury). Much of what we think we taste, we actually smell!

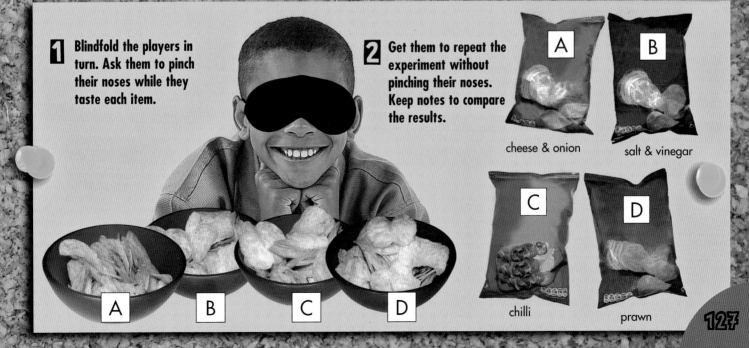

1 Blindfold the players in turn. Ask them to pinch their noses while they taste each item.

2 Get them to repeat the experiment without pinching their noses. Keep notes to compare the results.

A — cheese & onion
B — salt & vinegar
C — chilli
D — prawn

A B C D